COURTROOM SURVIVAL: MAKING THE TRAFFIC OFFICER A POWERFUL WITNESS
1999 EDITION

ORDER TODAY!

✉ **MAIL this coupon**
(include corrected address)

📠 **FAX this completed order form**
toll-free to 800/643-1280

☎ **Call toll-free 800/562-1197**

🖱 **ORDER ON-LINE at**
www.lexislawpublishing.com

LEXIS® LAW PUBLISHING
Attn: Customer Support
P.O. Box 7587
Charlottesville, VA 22906-7587

❏ Yes! Please send ____ copies of **Courtroom Survival: Making the Traffic Officer A Powerful Witness, 1999 Edition.** (37580-10)

30-Day Return Option: I may return my purchase within 30 days without obligation if not completely satisfied. All future supplementation, revisions, and related material will be sent automatically to me upon publication with the same return privileges.

❏ Payment enclosed
❏ Charge my ❏ VISA ❏ MasterCard ❏ AMEX

Account Number _____ Exp. Date _____

❏ Bill me ❏ Bill my firm
(Plus shipping and handling. Net 30 days)

❏ Send me your current LEXIS Law Publishing catalog

Your signature and customer number, if available, will ensure efficient handling of your order.

Signature _____ Phone # _____

Customer #** _____

Name _____

Address _____

City _____ State _____ Zip _____

* Plus sales tax, shipping and handling where applicable. Prices subject to change without notice.
**Your customer number appears on all past statements and invoices.

CBO 9/99

ESSENTIAL GUIDES FOR TRAFFIC OFFICERS

New edition!
Officer's DUI Handbook, 1999 Edition

John B. Kwasnoski, Gerald N. Partridge, John A. Stephen

NOW WITH CASES EXAMPLES

Officer's DUI Handbook contains practical advice for police officers about how to handle the arrest, investigation, and trial of an individual found guilty of driving under the influence of alcohol. Tips and checklists include:

- Checklists to aid in DUI investigations
- Arrest and custody issues
- Landmines to avoid during investigation
- Accident reconstruction checklists
- Tips to increase conviction rates
- How to testify
- New! Drug recognition evaluation

$25
Softbound, item #37553-11, ©1999

New audiotape series!
Legal and Practical Aspects of DUI/DWI

John A. Stephen

Listen to these audiotapes while traveling in your car, working in your office, or sitting at home! This new training tool helps police officers and investigators win convictions in DUI/DWI cases.

Summary Table of Contents
Section 1: The implied consent law
Section 2: Detection and apprehension
Section 3: The implied consent law and the administration of chemical tests
Section 4: Constitutional law in the DUI/DWI case

$100
Set of 5 audiotapes and table of cases, item #37585-10, ©1999

New!
COURTROOM SURVIVAL: Making the Traffic Officer a Powerful Witness

John B. Kwasnoski, Gerald N. Partridge, John A. Stephen

Learn about the elements of a winning criminal case and how law enforcement officers can use a powerful testimony to generate momentum in favor of the prosecution. Topics include:

- Preparing the traffic officer
- Preparing the prosecutor
- Stages of witness preparation
- Structure of the direct examination
- The three goals of a witness during cross-exam
- How to tell winners from losers
- How to investigate the defense attorney
- The four realities of cross-examination
- How the defense attorney controls you
- Profile of a competent police witness

$25
1 volume, softbound, item #37580-10, ©1999

Order Today!

Call toll-free at **800/562-1197**
Fax your order toll-free at **800/643-1280**
Order online at:
www.lexislawpublishing.com

LEXIS Publishing™

LEXIS®-NEXIS® • MARTINDALE-HUBBELL®
MATTHEW BENDER® • MICHIE™ • SHEPARD'S®

LEXIS, NEXIS and Martindale-Hubbell are registered trademarks and LEXIS Publishing and MICHIE are trademarks of Reed Elsevier Properties Inc., used under license. SHEPARD'S is a registered trademark of SHEPARD'S Company. Matthew Bender is a registered trademark of Matthew Bender Properties Inc. © 1999 LEXIS Law Publishing, a division of Reed Elsevier Inc. All rights reserved.

CRIMINAL AND TRAFFIC LAW SERIES

COURTROOM SURVIVAL: MAKING THE TRAFFIC OFFICER A POWERFUL WITNESS

John B. Kwasnoski
Gerald N. Partridge
John A. Stephen

LEXIS® LAW PUBLISHING
CHARLOTTESVILLE, VIRGINIA

COPYRIGHT © 1999
BY
LEXIS® LAW PUBLISHING
A Division of Reed Elsevier Inc.

Library of Congress Catalog Card No. 99-66626
ISBN 0-327-04950-2

All rights reserved.

3758010

TABLE OF CONTENTS

	Page
Scope	vii
Introduction	ix
About the Authors	xi

Chapter 1

BASIC PRINCIPLES OF COURTROOM TESTIFYING

§ 1-1. The Value of Truth 1
§ 1-2. The Bedrock for All Effective Testimony — Credibility 2
    § 1-2(a). Likeability 3
    § 1-2(b). Competency 4
    § 1-2(c). Honesty 5
§ 1-3. The Most Important of All Witness Skills — Visualization 5

Chapter 2

WITNESS PREPARATION

§ 2-1. Bad Investigations Make Bad Police Witnesses 7
§ 2-2. The Basic Elements of a Police Report 9
§ 2-3. Working With the Prosecutor 9
§ 2-4. Pre-Trial Police-Prosecutor Meeting 10
    § 2-4(a). Review Police Report Before Meeting 10
    § 2-4(b). The Witness Preparation Conference 12
    § 2-4(c). Visiting Crime Scene 13
    § 2-4(d). Exhibits 13
        § 2-4(d)(1). Real Evidence 14
        § 2-4(d)(2). Demonstrative Evidence 14
    § 2-4(e). The Structure of a Direct Examination 15
    § 2-4(f). Practicing Direct Examination 17
    § 2-4(g). Preparing for Cross-Examination 17
    § 2-4(h). Redirect Examination 19
    § 2-4(i). Officer at Counsel Table During Trial 19
    § 2-4(j). Witness Checklist 20

Chapter 3

DIRECT EXAMINATION

§ 3-1. Direct Examination Testimony Must First Be Credible 24
§ 3-2. Direct Examination — Goals 24
§ 3-3. Direct Examination Question Strings for Traffic Officers 25
§ 3-4. Elevating Quality of Police Officer's Testimony 37

TABLE OF CONTENTS

Page

§ 3-4(a). Special Training and Experience 37
§ 3-4(b). Measurement Accuracy and Completeness 41
§ 3-4(c). Basis for Reconstruction, SFST, and DRE Methodologies 46
§ 3-4(d). Certainty of Opinion Testimony 49
§ 3-5. Photographic and Videotape Evidence 51
    § 3-5(a). Lens 51
    § 3-5(b). Full Frame 51
    § 3-5(c). Including All Perspectives 51
    § 3-5(d). Photograph Details 52
    § 3-5(e). Using a Filter 52
    § 3-5(f). Photograph Investigators 52
    § 3-5(g). Photograph Log 52
    § 3-5(h). Digital Photographs 53
    § 3-5(i). Videotape Evidence 53
§ 3-6. Picking Fruits of "Credibility Tree" 53
    § 3-6(a). Calibration and Accuracy of Equipment 54
    § 3-6(b). Walking Scene to Look for Potentially Exculpatory
                Evidence 54
    § 3-6(c). Documenting Witness Locations on Drawings of Scene 54
    § 3-6(d). Prior Investigations Where No Charges Brought 55
    § 3-6(e). Consultations With Other Departments 55
    § 3-6(f). Description of Reference Point Used for Measurements 55
    § 3-6(g). Additional Measurements Not Used in Analysis of Crash 55
    § 3-6(h). Multiple Measurements of Evidence, With Values Most
                Favorable to Defendant, Used in All Calculations 56
    § 3-6(i). Drawing(s) of Scene Verified by Actual Measurements 56
    § 3-6(j). Going Back to Scene of Nighttime Crash During Daylight
                Hours 57
    § 3-6(k). Use of Models to Show Jury How Crash Occurred 58
    § 3-6(*l*). Inspection of Deflated Tires and Coinciding Road
                Evidence 58
§ 3-7. Inoculation Against Defense Attacks 59
    § 3-7(a). Omissions in Evidence Gathering or Documentation 59
    § 3-7(b). Expert's Opinion Differs From Testimony of Civilian
                Witness 60
    § 3-7(c). Calculations Could Not Be Corroborated 61
    § 3-7(d). Reconstructionist Not Present at Scene 62
    § 3-7(e). Witness a Crash Reconstructionist Not Expert in Other
                Areas 62
    § 3-7(f). No Statement From Defendant 63

TABLE OF CONTENTS

Page

§ 3-7(g). Unprepared Witness 63
§ 3-7(h). No Tests Performed on Vehicles Involved in Crash 64

Chapter 4

CROSS EXAMINATION

§ 4-1. Cross-Examination — What the Police Witness Needs to Know 67
§ 4-2. Cross-Examinations Dictate Case Outcomes 67
§ 4-3. Two Types of Cross-Examination 69
   § 4-3(a). General Areas of Attack on Police Witnesses 70
   § 4-3(b). Attacking the Police Witness' Perception and/or Memory of an Event 70
   § 4-3(c). Prior Inconsistent Statements 71
   § 4-3(d). Bias, Prejudice, and Motivation 71
   § 4-3(e). Incompetence 71
§ 4-4. Specific Attack Strategies for Traffic Officers 71
§ 4-5. Attack Strategies Commonly Used Against Drug Recognition Experts ... 72
§ 4-6. Common Attacks on Police Accident Reconstructionists 72
§ 4-7. Control 73
   § 4-7(a). The Use of Leading Questions 74
   § 4-7(b). The Use of Headlines 74
   § 4-7(c). Interrupting the Witness 74
   § 4-7(d). Intimidation 75
   § 4-7(e). Using the Judge 75
   § 4-7(f). Use of a Document 75
§ 4-8. Witness Strategies to Counter the Cross-Examination 75
   § 4-8(a). Witness Control of Time 76
   § 4-8(b). Defense Attorney Incompetence 77
      § 4-8(b)(1). When Defense Attorney Fails to Listen 77
      § 4-8(b)(2). When Defense Attorney Lacks Questioning Capacity 77
   § 4-8(c). Applying Visualization in Cross-Examination 77
§ 4-9. In-Depth Analysis of Strategies Used in Reconstruction 78
   § 4-9(a). Witness Knowledge/Competency 78
   § 4-9(b). Incomplete or Faulty Investigation 84
   § 4-9(c). Errors in Investigation or Reconstruction 96
   § 4-9(d). Attacks on the Certainty of Opinion(s) 102

TABLE OF CONTENTS

APPENDICES

Page

Appendix A: Accident Reconstruction Associations 109
Appendix B: Computer-Generated Evidence 111
Appendix C: Impairment at Low Blood Alcohol Concentrations —
    Driving Skills Associated with Observations that
    Trigger the Traffic Stop 117
Appendix D: Impairment at Low Blood Alcohol Concentrations —
    Skills Associated with Observations During Field
    Sobriety Tests 121

Additional Resources 123

SCOPE

Courtroom Survival: Making the Traffic Officer a Powerful Witness is a "nuts and bolts" instruction book for police officers who want to become effective witnesses. While the practices and principles set forth in this book apply to all types of police officers, from the town marshall to a specialized federal agent, there has been a conscious choice to focus on police officers involved in traffic situations. There are several reasons for this choice:

1. Most police officers start their careers as patrol officers. If they learn successful testifying techniques early enough in their careers, they can apply the skills developed as traffic officers to become outstanding witnesses in whatever type of case they may investigate.

2. Traffic cases pose the full range of typical courtroom challenges for the police witness. All of the principles of testifying set forth in this book apply with equal force to the full range of law enforcement professionals.

3. Patrol officers spend more time in court than any other type of officer.

Chapter One introduces the basic principles and the skills needed to be an effective and persuasive courtroom witness. Understanding the nature of truth and its relationship to reality, listening to questions, and the ability to visualize the scene and convey it to the courtroom are essential. Trial tips throughout this chapter and the remainder of the book provide important practical advice. These "tips" reinforce the text and help the officer fine tune his/her trial testimony.

Chapter Two focuses on the steps involved in witness preparation. It is in the "preparation" stage that trials are won or lost. The necessity of a complete investigation that is competently documented is emphasized. The remainder of the chapter is devoted to how the police officer and prosecutor can most effectively work together to prepare the police-witness for trial. A comprehensive witness checklist is provided.

Chapter Three is devoted to the form and content of the direct examination. Sample direct examinations illustrate how an examination proceeds from introductory questions that simply acquaint the jury with the police-witness, to the qualifications of the officer to testify in the case, and finally to the substance of his/her testimony. Question strings are provided specifically for the traffic situation, but can be modified to fit specific case facts for use by any police-witness, from a drug task force officer to a homicide investigator. The structure of the direct examination is logical and purposeful, and once the witness understands it, the testimony within the direct examination can be more convincingly presented. The concept of inoculating the witness against expected defense attacks is introduced. The use of exhibits to reinforce the witness' story of the case finalizes "painting the picture" for the jury, and the need for planning the use of exhibits during the pre-trial preparation of the case is stressed. Anticipation of the defense attorney's methods of cross examination is discussed. An in-depth presentation and analysis of the direct examination of a police witness, an accident reconstructionist, is provided, with explanations.

Chapter Four is devoted to cross examination. Included are extensive listings of attack strategies and witness control employed by defense attorneys. As in Chapter Three, an in-depth analysis is provided of defense attacks on a police-witness, again an accident reconstructionist, taken from actual trial situations. The analysis and commentary on these defense strategies provides invaluable insight for all police-witnesses who wish to anticipate how their own testimony might be attacked.

Extended appendices are provided in the following areas: **Appendix A**: Accident Reconstruction Associations, **Appendix B**: Computer Generated Evidence, **Appendix C**: Impairment at Low Blood Alcohol Concentrations — Driving Skills Associated with the Observations that Trigger the Traffic Stop, **Appendix D**: Impairment at Low Blood Alcohol Concentrations — Skills Associated with Observations During the Field Sobriety Tests.

INTRODUCTION

Most officers have been trained in certain critical skills: to make observations, to conduct interviews, to document evidence, and to write complete reports — skills that are absolutely essential to the success of any case. Because traffic violations and traffic crashes occur with such frequency, it is common for traffic officers to become highly proficient in these investigative and reporting skills. And because the majority of criminal cases are resolved through plea agreements, an officer may only infrequently be called as a witness. Ironically, with so much at stake, more effort is made to ensure that officers make complete and compelling accounts in their reports than to prepare them for testifying to the same matters in front of a jury, where all of their prior efforts are put to the test.

Probably the most important challenge for police officers who have competently performed their work in the investigative stage of the case, whether it led them to simply issuing a traffic ticket or to arresting a defendant for a vehicular homicide, is to deliver an account of their activities and observations through courtroom testimony to jury in a clear and compelling manner. For many reasons, not the least of which is the pressure of having a defense attorney whose oath requires a zealous representation of the defendant and attacking the police-witness' competency and credibility, being a witness is one of the most difficult and most demanding aspects of a police officer's job. In the pressure-cooker environment of a courtroom all of the excellent investigative work of an officer can be negated in a moment's mental lapse on the witness stand.

If you were to ask a seasoned police officer who has testified numerous times how he/she became a good witness, most would tell you that it was in the school of hard knocks, learning by experiences that were sometimes uncomfortable or even hurtful. Most would tell of experiences in which the jury misunderstood or did not fully comprehend their testimony, or about times when the defense attorney was able to distort the reality that they had brought to the courtroom. Surely most would tell of a time when they had finished testifying, only to remember what should have been emphasized or clarified; but, of course, it was too late. There actually is free instruction on being a good witness available to police officers nearly every day of the week at the local courthouse in the form of very qualified and experienced witnesses, the best of whom are often privately retained experts testifying in civil trials. In these trials, the officer can observe skilled trial attorneys vigorously examining witnesses and can soon discern a pattern to the attorney's questioning and tactics and a structure to the entire trial.

But for those officers who do not wish to go through the pain and labor of years of trial and error, and do not have the luxury of time to sit in courthouses on their days off, the authors through this short book have tried to shorten the learning process. The wisdom drawn from the experiences of many others can be adopted as your own so that you can become a better witness.

This book accelerates the motivated traffic officer's learning curve in the area of being a persuasive witness. For efficiency throughout the book, it will be presumed that officers are testifying in front of juries, even though many, if not most, of a traffic officer's cases are tried by judge.

ABOUT THE AUTHORS

John B. Kwasnoski is a Professor of Forensic Physics at Western New England College. He has completed more than 500 accident reconstructions and testified throughout the country in criminal and civil cases, including the Susan Smith case in Union, South Carolina. He has written extensively on accident investigation and trial techniques, and he lectures nationwide before police officers on DUI issues. He is also co-author of the bestselling *Investigation and Prosecution of DWI and Vehicular Homicide*, published by LEXIS® Law Publishing, for use by police officers and prosecutors.

Gerald N. Partridge is a graduate of the University of Iowa College of Law. He retired from a career as a prosecuting attorney in 1997 to write and lecture. He is the Executive Director of Police Legal Sciences, Inc., a company that creates monthly computer-based police training lessons. He teaches witness preparation and cross examination for police and prosecutor agencies across the country, including for the National College of District Attorneys. He is a co-author of LEXIS® Law Publishing's *Investigation and Prosecution of DWI and Vehicular Homicide*.

John A. Stephen is an Assistant Commissioner of the New Hampshire Department of Safety and has served as Assistant Attorney General in the New Hampshire Department of Justice, where his primary responsibility was state-wide coordination of DWI/vehicular homicide prosecution. Prior to that time, Mr. Stephen was an assistant county attorney prosecuting numerous jury and non-jury criminal trials. In addition to being a co-author of LEXIS® Law Publishing's *Investigation and Prosecution of DWI and Vehicular Homicide*, Mr. Stephen is the author of the highly regarded *New Hampshire DWI Manual*. He is also an instructor at the New Hampshire Police Academy.

Chapter 1

BASIC PRINCIPLES OF COURTROOM TESTIFYING

§ 1-1. The Value of Truth.
§ 1-2. The Bedrock for All Effective Testimony — Credibility.
    § 1-2(a). Likeability.
    § 1-2(b). Competency.
    § 1-2(c). Honesty.
§ 1-3. The Most Important of All Witness Skills — Visualization.

§ 1-1. The Value of Truth.

The outcome of every trial is dictated by what the jury believes to be the truth, and in non-jury cases by what the judge believes to be the truth. The truth is delivered in a courtroom in the form of evidence. The evidence can be delivered in the form of testimony or in the form of exhibits. What testimony and what exhibits are allowed to be considered by the jury (or judge) are governed by the rules of evidence. In applying these rules of evidence during a trial, the judge has an obligation which, in all federal courts and most state courts, reads:

> These rules shall be construed ... to the end that the truth may be ascertained....

Federal Rule of Evidence 102

All witnesses that enter a courtroom must swear or affirm that they will tell the truth. The first step for a police officer to become a powerful witness is to understand and appreciate the relationship of truth to objective reality.

Consider the old and well-known children's story about three blind men.

> *Three blind men unexpectedly found their path blocked by an obstacle they were sure they had never before encountered. They each touched it with their hands to try to determine its identity. One announced that the obstacle was simply a thick, tightly wound rope tied to a large rock. Another, not realizing he was touching the leg of an animal, claimed the object was a tree and they were standing at its base. The third blind man barely touched the animal's trunk before jumping back, screaming that a huge python snake was dangling in the path.*

Which of them was telling the truth? If we can assume that they were each sincerely reporting a fact about the reality they were experiencing, then they were all telling the truth. <u>Truth is simply the earnest effort to describe reality</u>. When people simply and sincerely report their observations of an event, the facts of that particular event, they are being truthful. When enough facts of an event are assembled, the objective reality of the event is knowable.

Nothing is more persuasive to jurors than the recognition of objective reality. At whatever point in a trial the jurors conclude what actually happened in the case, all interpretations of the evidence before and after that point will be adjusted until they conform to the jurors' conclusion. When the witnesses are able to bring the objective reality of a criminal event into a courtroom, all other tactics and strategies of persuasion inconsistent with that reality become ineffective.

The fictitious L.A. Detective, Jack Webb, provided a model description of what police officers everywhere do when he said: "All we want are the facts, ma'am, nothing but the facts." The facts which the police gather, when presented effectively in a courtroom, will lead the jurors to know reality and to base their decisions on that reality.

Trial Tip

The goal of the police witness must be to provide fact upon fact about an event, in the form of a story, to illuminate the police witness' investigation in the minds of the jurors.

The courtroom in criminal cases was built as a place where a civilized society could hold the guilty accountable and protect the innocent from harm. To do that, someone must be a bearer of truth, an accurate reporter of objective reality. That role in the vast majority of cases falls to the police officer. Without that police witness there would not be a case, there would not be a trial, and there would not be a need for jurors, a judge, or attorneys.

§ 1-2. The Bedrock for All Effective Testimony — Credibility.

All trials are about credibility — about who the jury believes. Credibility is a prerequisite to persuasion. The police witness must be accepted as a credible reporter of facts.

How does the police witness establish credibility? Reduced to its basics, whether the jurors find a police witness credible depends on:

- whether they like the officer;
- whether they believe the officer is competent; and
- whether they believe the officer is honest.

> **Trial Tip**
>
> *The most important factor in whether the police witness will be believed is whether the jurors like the officer.*

§ 1-2(a). Likeability.

While a friendly attitude and a conversational style both help promote likeabililty, it is essential that very early in an officer's direct examination a more concrete effort be made to "humanize" the officer to the jury. The police uniform is an asset in terms of promoting the perception of competency. It is sometimes a liability in terms of making the officer likeable. Many jurors' closest and most recent contacts with a police officer may have been negative. It may have been in the context of receiving a traffic citation or a police response to a no-win domestic violence situation. The police witness must be individualized, humanized, and distinguished from all other officers.

> **Trial Tip**
>
> *At some point before trial, the police witness should discuss with the prosecutor enough details of his or her private life that in the early stages of the direct examination, the prosecutor can introduce those details in order to help the officer establish a common bond with jurors: length of time residing in the community, attending/graduating from a local school, being a parent, being a grandparent, coaching, scouting, working with children or the elderly, fundraising, membership in local service clubs or churches, etc.*

Likeability is further advanced by the officer's patience, eye contact, calm and confident tone of voice, and pace. It is also strengthened when the jurors find the officer to be a person who is open and friendly, a person who cares about others, and a person with whom they have shared values. The jurors want such a person to always demonstrate fairness and objectivity.

Trial Tip

Objectivity vs. Advocacy. When testifying, a police witness must always tell the truth, the whole truth, and nothing but the truth. He/She must never appear to take on the role of advocating for a conviction. It is the prosecutor's role to advocate the conviction.

---

§ 1-2(b). Competency.

Factors that strengthen the jurors' perception of the police witness as a competent individual include whether he or she:

- projects a well-groomed appearance;
- has good posture;
- has a clean, well-pressed uniform (or suit);
- has prepared a report in the case;
- listens well to whomever is speaking;
- maintains eye contact with the attorneys when listening to questions and with jurors when giving a lengthy answer or using an exhibit;
- speaks clearly using an easily understood vocabulary;
- handles court exhibits without distracting mannerisms;
- uses clear, visual images during testimony;
- demonstrates pride and thoroughness when describing his or her work; and
- offers explanations of special technical terms relative to the work in the case, so jurors aren't confused or offended.

The early phase of the direct examination is where qualifying questions are posited to the police witness and the impression of competency can be solidified. Any special training, recognition, or distinguished experiences should be noted, emphasizing and distinguishing the witness' credentials as they relate to the particular type of case being prosecuted. Where possible, the officer should modestly acknowledge any qualifications that distinguish him or her from other officers in the department.

Trial Tip

The officer should inform the prosecutor prior to trial of his/her years of experience, education, training, honors, awards, and the number of investigations of crashes (like the one that occurred in the case being tried) that he/she has conducted and/or participated in.

§ 1-2(c). Honesty.

The quality of honesty can be measured by the degree to which a witness appears to be willing to disclose information, particularly during the cross-examination phase. A police witness does not need to be successfully impeached to lose credibility points with a jury. Exhibiting evasiveness and hostility during questioning by the defense attorney is a common way police witnesses can self-destruct. An admission of a shortcoming made during the direct examination, with an appropriate explanation of its importance to the case, can establish the honesty of the police witness.

§ 1-3. The Most Important of All Witness Skills — Visualization.

The persuasive force that objective reality has in the courtroom has already been described. The mental activity that best succeeds in comprehending objective reality is the act of visualizing. When jurors visualize a witness' testimony, they are gathering and grasping the facts of the case. When they visualize enough of the facts, they can grasp the reality of the event being described. When they grasp the reality of the event, they cannot be dislodged and their decisions will be based on their perception of reality. Before witnesses can convey clear visual images, they must testify from their original visual recollection of the event they are reporting.

Trial Tip

To succeed, a police witness must make a conscious and continuous effort to visualize his or her testimony as it is being given. Every aspect of the witness' courtroom testimony that the jurors hear should have a visual counterpart in the witness' mind's eye.

This internal/external aspect of effective testimony often generates the following:

- a chronological order;
- a story line;
- action;
- a perspective (usually the witness' point of view); and
- a rationale for why the witness took a particular action

Unlike the left to right, sequential limits of the written word, visualizing is a right brain activity that allows a witness to apply his or her best mental faculties to activating the jurors' best mental faculties to the examination of the facts being presented. Visualizing in this manner allows the officer to overcome the tendency to make associations to memories of unrelated events. Once a witness has formed a clear mental picture, it is extremely difficult to develop an answer to any question that does not fit the picture. The visual picture becomes a filter through which all questions are passed, and from which all responses are generated. Visualizing is effective on both direct and cross-examination. It has the effect of forcing the witness to select only the words from his or her vocabulary that accurately describe the visual image. On direct examination, the witness will be an extremely accurate reporter of the facts. On cross-examination, any effort to invite or to force a witness to change the vocabulary or distort the mental image is easily rebuffed.

In addition, visualizing reduces the tendency for voluntary speculation by the witness. Visualizing allows a witness to see the limits of his or her knowledge of any event with great clarity. Limits generally fall into three categories:

(1) Matters about which the witness is certain, where no one and nothing should make him or her budge;
(2) Matters about which the witness has no knowledge or no recollection; and
(3) Matters where the witness has overall certainty about an observation, but has no reasonable basis for recollecting minute details: exact words, distances, speeds, and times.

Trial Tip

No defense attorney can succeed in distorting the testimony of a police witness who has conducted a competent investigation, prepared a complete report, and visualizes his or her courtroom testimony.

Chapter 2

WITNESS PREPARATION

§ 2-1. Bad Investigations Make Bad Police Witnesses.
§ 2-2. The Basic Elements of a Police Report.
§ 2-3. Working With the Prosecutor.
§ 2-4. Pre-Trial Police-Prosecutor Meeting.
    § 2-4(a). Review Police Report Before Meeting.
    § 2-4(b). The Witness Preparation Conference.
    § 2-4(c). Visiting Crime Scene.
    § 2-4(d). Exhibits.
        § 2-4(d)(1). Real Evidence.
        § 2-4(d)(2). Demonstrative Evidence.
    § 2-4(e). The Structure of a Direct Examination.
    § 2-4(f). Practicing Direct Examination.
    § 2-4(g). Preparing for Cross-Examination.
    § 2-4(h). Redirect Examination.
    § 2-4(i). Officer at Counsel Table During Trial.
    § 2-4(j). Witness Checklist.

§ 2-1. Bad Investigations Make Bad Police Witnesses.

The purpose of this book is to teach police officers how to be confident, effective, and successful courtroom witnesses. To become such a witness, the police officer must first conduct competent, effective, and thorough investigations, and document them in complete and well-written reports. To use a common phrase: "You can't make a silk purse out of a sow's ear." An officer who fails in his or her duty to conduct a proper investigation is "out of position" to present successful courtroom testimony.

In light of the importance the quality of the investigation has to the courtroom, there is perhaps no more valuable time for the police officer to begin thinking about preparing trial testimony than while still in the investigative stage of the case. With each step in any investigation the officer is well-advised to ask two questions: "Is this an action a good police officer would take?" and/or "Would a failure to take this action reflect laziness or incompetence?" The officer never wants to be on the low road on the witness stand — offering explanations and excuses for what was done or not done months earlier when the case was investigated.

Officers would do well to presume that with every ticket they issue, every charge they file, and every arrest they make, the defendant will hire an attorney and the case will go to trial. From that perspective they can better appreciate:

- that it is the defense attorney's job to identify a defense theory for the client;

- that every criminal case has available to it at least one defense theory;
- that the defense theory will effectively remove all blame or culpability from the defendant; and
- that the seeds of the defense theory are planted each time the police officer leaves something undone or performs some required action badly during his or her investigation.

Consider the collision of two vehicles where one driver, the defendant, obviously crossed the centerline. Unless the officer considers the defense perspective and fills some of the gaps in the story line of the case, several defenses emerge:

- a mechanical defect,
- an animal crossing the road, or
- the erratic driving by the victim in the oncoming vehicle;

are all potential defense theories.

Consider a *per se* driving while impaired or intoxicated case where the critical evidence against the defendant is the intoxilyzer result. If the defendant's drinking companions aren't interviewed at the time of the defendant's arrest, the defense can use them to testify as to the number of drinks the defendant had, the type of drinks, and the number of hours over which the drinking occurred. Absent successful cross-examination or available rebuttal evidence, the companions' testimony would have some weight with the jury. Its real value, however, is the basis for a hypothetical question about what the defendant's BAC would have been using the companions' numbers. The answer to that question may be a very different number from what the state's intoxilyzer showed. The testimony from a professional toxicologist will carry a great deal of weight with the jury, especially if the testimony was extracted from the state's own toxicologist.

Vehicular homicide (or negligent homicide) cases, where securing crime scenes, gathering physical evidence, and interviewing witnesses (including the defendant) take a backseat to saving human life, are very susceptible to a variety of defense theories and claims: that the defendant was not the driver of the vehicle; that the victim had been in the oncoming lane and swerved at the same time as the defendant, leaving everyone in the victim's correct lane; that alcohol was not the proximate cause of the crash. These claims would seem absurd, except that months after the investigation is closed, the claims cannot be disproved.

> **Trial Tip**
>
> *The sooner in an investigation the police officer begins considering and eliminating defense theories, the better witness he or she will make when the case reaches trial.*

§ 2-2. The Basic Elements of a Police Report.

Almost as valuable as the investigation itself is the officer's documentation of the investigation. Later portions of this book are devoted very specifically to the investigation and documentation of traffic investigations. It is sufficient at this point to identify the basic elements of a police report as including:

- a narrative of the officer's activities;
- witness interviews;
- statements of the defendant;
- physical evidence seized; and
- additional investigative materials: photos, diagrams, criminal histories, driving records, special forms.

§ 2-3. Working With the Prosecutor.

The closer the working relationship a police officer has with the prosecuting attorney for his case, the better witness in that case he or she is more likely to be. At a minimum there should be some basis for mutual trust between attorney and witness. The prosecutor is largely responsible for that. Many things in a trial cannot be planned for, but by working together, these two professionals can avoid either sabotaging their own case or becoming victims of defense land mines.

Jurors perceive police and prosecutors operating in the courtroom and believe they operate and interact in the same manner as a team does. That is rarely true. Most often the officer and the prosecutor communicate for a few minutes in a hallway before the officer is called into the courtroom to begin testifying.

Outside of situations where police and prosecutor are members of the same task force, the idea of the two working together the way a team functions is often not achievable. "Aligning" the police and prosecutor effort is a more realistic prospect. Alignment occurs when the prosecutor helps the police officer understand the case from the perspective of the courtroom, or when the police officer helps the prosecutor orient his or her perspective to that of the police-investigator. The police officer who can establish "alignment" with the prosecutor can help the prosecutor recreate the police work product and the image of objective reality in the courtroom for the jury.

Trial Tip

Greater "alignment" occurs in jurisdictions where police have "ride along" programs that prosecuting attorneys utilize.

---

§ 2-4. Pre-Trial Police-Prosecutor Meeting.

Often the difference between winning and losing a case where a conviction is deserved is whether the police witness and prosecutor met before the trial began and prepared.

Trial Tip

If the prosecutor fails to arrange a pre-trial meeting with the police-witness, it is appropriate and necessary that the officer arranges an appointment with the prosecutor.

---

§ 2-4(a). Review Police Report Before Meeting.

Before meeting with the prosecutor, the officer should review the case report.

Officers should read through the report, visualizing each step of the investigation and the manner in which it is portrayed in the report. In important cases, the officer can fortify the visualization process by returning to the location of the investigation, physically retracing the same steps that were taken in first gathering the evidence in the case.

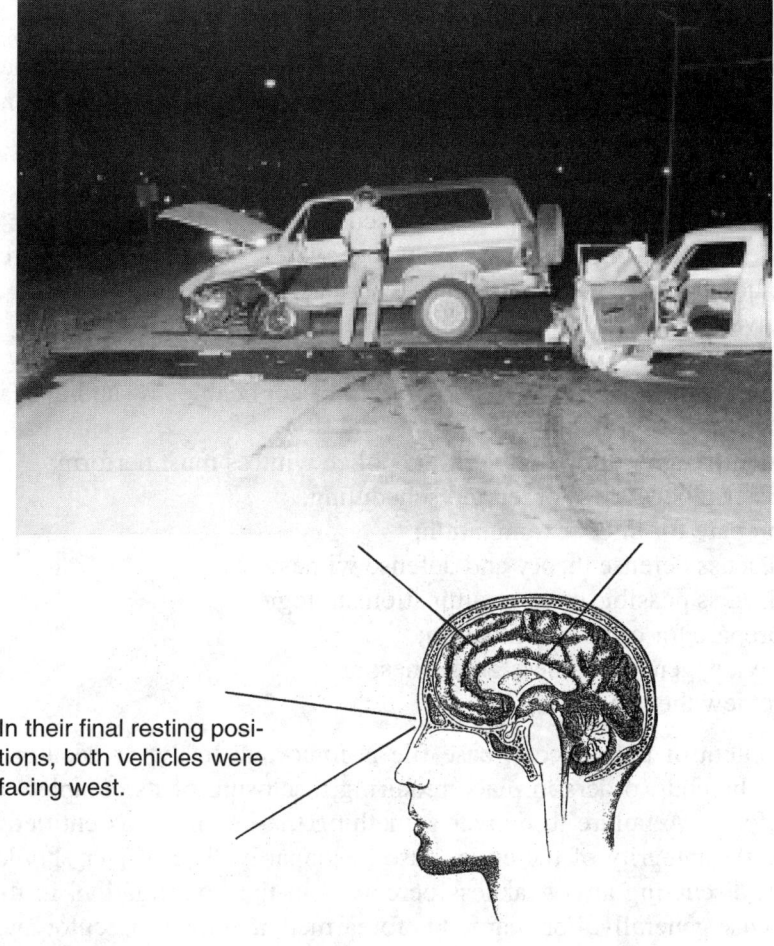

In their final resting positions, both vehicles were facing west.

Visualizing the written report.

He or she should do this with the mindset that the defense attorney has spent more hours studying it than the officer took to write it. If the attorney can trip an officer up with his own words, from his own report, the officer will lose credibility. He or she will no longer be considered truthful, "facts" will disappear, and nothing will be left on which the jury can grasp what really happened in the case. Ensuring that each word and phrase has a corresponding visual counterpart in the police-witness' mind's eye virtually eliminates the prospect that the witness can be tripped up by what has been written in the report.

§ 2-4(b). The Witness Preparation Conference.

A witness conference can cover a wide range of trial preparation issues. If the officer were the chief investigator in a case, it would not be uncommon for the following general list of topics to be covered:

- review with the prosecutor the entire contents of the case file;
- review the officer's report and discuss weaknesses;
- identify and discuss any newly discovered information in the case, including any reports on forensic tests;
- inventory and examine all physical evidence;
- identify and examine all other court exhibits;
- review the charging decision in light of applicable law and available evidence;
- identify any follow-up work the police witness must perform;
- determine witness order and scheduling;
- prepare for direct examination;
- discuss defense theory and defense witnesses;
- discuss possible cross-examination strategies;
- prepare for cross-examination;
- review general witness guidelines; and
- review the jury list.

The content of the officer's case file is important to the prosecutor because there may be court orders in place requiring disclosure of its complete contents to the defense. A failure to deliver something the defense was entitled to have can place the integrity of the entire case in jeopardy. The officer should not be shy about discussing any weakness perceived in the investigation, in the report or in the case generally. Forewarned is forearmed, and the prosecutor and officer can discuss strategies to address weaknesses.

Whether the officer appears competent in court is often determined by how well the officer handles exhibits. Fumbling or appearing confused about an important exhibit is unforgivable. The officer should know where he or she placed identifying marks or tags or stickers on each piece of evidence. He/she must also be familiar with every exhibit the prosecutor intends for the officer to use while testifying. The prosecutor needs to learn from the officer as much as the officer can relate about each item of physical evidence in the case.

Using the police report and exhibits, the police officer and prosecutor should walk chronologically through the investigation. Along the way, the prosecutor may assume the role of "devil's advocate" to try to identify weaknesses or vulnerabilities in the officer's investigation. Typical areas of inquiry would include the following:

- the officer's understanding of the technical and legal aspects of the case;
- the officer's ability to explain special terms in layman's terms;
- areas of perceived incompleteness in the investigation and any explanations the officer may provide;
- the witness' level of certainty about observations and opinions;
- the extent to which the officer is self-conscious about his or her level of formal education, training or experience; and
- the amount of courtroom experience the officer has had.

An officer should not take these inquiries personally. It is best that the prosecutor uncover as many potential problems as possible before the trial, than to risk a fatal attack on the witness in front of the jury by a hostile and relentless defense attorney during cross-examination.

With regard to technical or legal aspects of the case, the officer should make use of the prosecutor's legal expertise. A police witness may have sufficient knowledge of the law to properly charge a defendant, but it is a good idea to ask the prosecutor to clarify what the elements are that must be proven. An inadvertent or improper use of a term of law by the officer may give the jurors the wrong impression of the legal aspect of the case, and if such an error is significant it may become the focus of the defense attorney's argument to the jury.

With due regard to identifying and anticipating problem areas in the case, the majority of pre-trial time with the prosecutor should be spent preparing the prosecutor and the police witness for the direct examination.

§ 2-4(c). Visiting Crime Scene.

The fastest and most effective way of ensuring that the prosecutor is on the same page with the police officer is to walk through the officer's report at the crime scene. In the more important and complex cases, the officer should politely, but aggressively, encourage the prosecutor to conduct this activity. When the prosecutor can see the case through the eyes of the police witness, everything about the prosecutor's courtroom presentation will be strengthened, including the direct examination of the police witness. During the time spent at the scene, it is common for ideas for exhibits and demonstrations and key questions to germinate.

§ 2-4(d). Exhibits.

The officer and the prosecutor should spend whatever time is necessary to discuss the most effective way the officer's testimony can be presented in the courtroom. Exhibits play a significant role in the effort to clarify the officer's testimony.

Over time, officers identify certain types of exhibits or certain demonstrations that they rely on when they testify. The officer needs to express his/her thoughts about exhibits to the prosecutor to gain the prosecutor's support and cooperation. The timing of the use of the exhibit within the framework of the direct examination, the location of the evidence or exhibit sticker, and how the exhibit will be "published" or exhibited to the jury are issues that must be carefully reviewed and rehearsed between the prosecutor and police witness.

Exhibits fall within one of two categories of evidence in a case: real and demonstrative.

§ 2-4(d)(1). Real Evidence.

Real evidence is a physical object or document that is an actual piece of the "reality" of the case. Real evidence, by its nature, tends to elevate the prosecutor's version of the facts. The care with which jurors consistently handle a piece of real evidence demonstrates the high value they place on tangible evidence that they can touch and evaluate during the trial. The officer's ability to persuade increases each time the officer ties his or her testimony to real evidence.

Trial Tip

Officers should seize all available physical evidence at the scene that might help the jury understand the event.

§ 2-4(d)(2). Demonstrative Evidence.

Demonstrative evidence is a visual aid that has been designed and created to support the prosecutor's version of events. Demonstrative evidence should be highly visible and simplified. Jurors need to completely understand an exhibit and the reason for its introduction. The availability and use of demonstrative evidence to enhance communication with the jury is limited only by the imagination of the prosecutor and witness and the discretion of the judge.

Trial Tip

The witness should practice any steps required for publishing the exhibit to the jury. Obtaining permission from the judge to step down from the witness chair and approach the jury to publish the photographs will place the witness very close to the jury, often resulting in greater acceptance of the witness by certain jurors.

§ 2-4(e). The Structure of a Direct Examination.

The prosecutor has virtually complete control over how the direct examination of the police witness will be conducted. Most prosecutors, however, welcome suggestions and even assistance from some witnesses on how to best conduct the direct examination, so that the testimony from that witness can have the maximum persuasive impact on the jury. Expert witnesses are often asked by prosecutors to assist in the preparation of the direct examination.

Chapter 3 provides samples of typical direct examination question strings that could be used in appropriate traffic cases. For officers who have established sufficient rapport with their prosecutors to assist them in composing the direct examination, the samples in Chapter 3 are a good starting point. Officers with less opportunity for input may simply propose that the prosecutor use the following three-part structure for organizing the direct examination: First, let the police witness narrate his or her testimony without exhibits; second, ask the witness to respond to potential defense attacks in a way that diffuses their impact; and finally, highlight the police witness' testimony using the physical evidence, demonstrations, and visual aids. A brief discussion of each stage follows:

Part I. Introduction, Qualifications, and Narrating the Story

Part I is a line of questions that allows the officer to identify and distinguish himself or herself to the jury; establish his/her credibility; and tell a story from start to finish without any reference to exhibits. The value of the uninterrupted narrative is that the jury has the greatest opportunity to get to know the witness and follow the witness' story line — grasping the "big picture."

The examination should begin with a simple series of questions that allows the officer to gain control over his/her voice and breathing, to develop confidence that he/she will do a good job on the witness stand, and to settle into a conversational style of speaking — the same pace, rhythm, level of loudness, and vocabulary as the officer uses in everyday conversation with civilians.

An often-overlooked part of the direct examination is the qualifying questions asked of the police witness. The jury should not get the impression that the witness "is just like every other police officer," wearing a uniform, carrying a weapon, trained at an academy, and writing parking and traffic tickets. In order for the jury to place confidence in the witness' testimony, the witness should be "humanized" and, if possible, distinguished from the stereotypical police officer. The officer may already have written out some qualifying questions to assist the prosecutor. There is a direct correlation between the qualifying questions and the credibility that the jury attaches to the police witness' testimony. The importance of the qualifying questions should not be minimized or underestimated.

> **Trial Tip**
>
> *If the witness can establish a conversational style during the direct examination, the jurors will expect a similar non-evasive style during the cross-examination.*

Part II. The Inoculation Stage

At the second stage in the direct examination, potential defense attacks can be raised for the witness to respond to. If there exists damaging information in a case that can be used to weaken the police witness' credibility and make the police witness vulnerable to a cross-examination attack, the prosecutor has two choices: the prosecutor can leave the matter alone and leave it for the defense attorney to cross-examine the witness about, or the prosecutor can ask questions about the damaging information that will allow the witness an opportunity to put the damaging information into perspective or put a positive "spin" to the information. This technique of taking the sting out of a potential defense attack is called "inoculating the witness." If the prosecutor lets the defense attorney use the damaging information first, it will have a maximum impact on the jury. If the prosecutor and witness raise the matter first, it will have minimal impact on the jury. An analogy may be instructive:

There is a loaded gun sitting on the exhibit table during the direct examination, and in that gun is a bullet with the police witness' name on it. The prosecutor can pick up the gun, warn the police witness to duck out of the way, and then fire the gun over the head of the police witness, causing no harm. Or the loaded gun can be left laying on the table for the defense attorney to pick up during the cross-examination phase of the officer's testimony. If the defense attorney uses the gun, it can inflict a mortal wound to the officer and the case.

Through a combination of using non-inflammatory and "open-ended" questions, potential impeachment can be diffused before the defense uses it during cross-examination.

Part III. Exhibit and Demonstration Stage

Here important facts in the witness' earlier testimony can be emphasized using exhibits. When the police witness enters the courtroom, he/she should feel comfortable and look at ease. The witness should see the courtroom ahead of time and have a chance to form a mental image of where the jurors are located, how the witness box is situated, where the exhibits are kept, how exhibits will be displayed to the jury, etc. The witness should ask the prosecutor what the judge's policy is toward wearing a weapon into the courtroom, since it would be devastating to have the judge admonish the police witness in front of the jury. It is helpful and builds confidence in the witness to practice putting up the exhibits or using the chalkboard ahead of time. The witness should be aware of how the exhibits are marked so as not to fumble with identifying the exhibits during the testimony.

Trial Tip

The more closely the direct examination develops out of a collaborative effort between the prosecutor and the police witness, the more effective the presentation to the jury is likely to be.

---

§ 2-4(f). Practicing Direct Examination.

Some prosecutors write out their direct examinations for their witnesses word-for-word, removing any room for deviation at the time of trial. Others use a checklist of the items they wish to cover and the exhibits they intend to use with each witness. Whatever the prosecutor's style and however the direct examination is designed by the prosecutor, the officer and the prosecutor should go through the officer's testimony before they present it inside the courtroom. For the same reasons shipyards put their boats through a "shakedown" cruise, so that problems can be identified and corrected, pre-trial run-throughs of the direct examination allow adjustments and corrections to be made.

Trial Tip

Witness Preparation by Telephone. Effective witness preparation may be done by phone. Advantages of this method include: (1) it is faster and avoids interruptions; and (2) it promotes visualization by the witness. The disadvantage is that the witness and prosecutor have no opportunity to work through the exhibits together unless they do it at the courthouse.

---

§ 2-4(g). Preparing for Cross-Examination.

This is a very important area to discuss with the prosecutor. A police witness' testimony is only as valuable to a case as its capacity to withstand a cross-examination attack. Many police officers think that the cross-examination attacks by the defense attorney are personal in nature. Generally speaking, cross-examination attacks are not personal. The police witness may ask the prosecutor for assurances that if an attack does become personal that the prosecutor will lodge an objection with the judge and request the judge to impose some control over the questioning.

Trial Tip

The witness should not invite the prosecuting to demonstrate how a defense attorney might conduct the cross-examination. Even as a practice exercise, working relationships get bruised and confidence gets weakened.

Chapter 4 provides insight into a substantial number of potential defense strategies and tactics. The officer should ask the prosecutor to identify every potential area of attack he or she can imagine might be made under the facts of the case. With each possible or probable line of defense attack that is identified, the police officer should establish from the prosecutor whether the prosecutor intends on addressing the potentially damaging information on direct examination, through inoculation, or on redirect examination, if at all. It is valuable for the witness to know before he or she takes the stand exactly how the prosecutor intends to handle these vulnerable aspects of the witness' testimony. Ideally, the prosecutor can walk the witness through the identical inoculation questions he or she intends to ask the witness during the trial, or the identical questions the prosecutor intends to ask on redirect examination.

Trial Tip

Forewarned is forearmed. It is valuable for a witness to know as much as possible about the defense attorney's tactics and strategies.

Any pre-trial information about the experience level, skill level, and common tactics of the defense attorney in a case is helpful in promoting the officer's confidence on the witness stand. The police witness can ask other officers in the department about the defense attorney and what to expect, but the best source of information is likely to come from the prosecutor. The basic questions the officer wants answered are:

- How far will this defense attorney go in order to win the case?
- Does the attorney show a temper in the courtroom?

- Is the attorney a good listener?
- Is the attorney competent in the technical aspects of the case?
- Does the attorney have a pattern or a set routine for attacking police witnesses?

§ 2-4(h). Redirect Examination.

A definite portion of trial preparation should be devoted to redirect examination. Under the appropriate set of circumstances, and in the event the defense counsel's cross-examination weakens the credibility of the police witness, the prosecutor and witness should be prepared to respond with an effective redirect examination. An effective redirect examination allows the witness' last words to the jury be ones that help the state's side of the case. There are three types of situations where redirect examinations are appropriate and are easily accomplished:

1. Where the witness has requested, but was not permitted, to provide a more complete answer to a cross-examination question;
2. Where the prosecutor believes the defense attorney has generated a misleading implication that a very small fact in the case is of much greater importance than it actually is; and
3. Where the defense counsel has aggressively pursued a destructive cross-examination of the witness.

In the first situation, the prosecutor can simply review each instance where the witness expressed a need to expand an answer (and where it sufficiently advances the state's case) and ask a question that permits the witness to do so. In the second situation, the prosecutor should invite the witness to place the information the defense has highlighted into its proper perspective for the jury. In the third situation, the prosecutor can simply ask the witness whether, as a consequence to any matter raised through the cross-examination, the witness wishes to change any of his or her prior testimony.

§ 2-4(i). Officer at Counsel Table During Trial.

Most jurisdictions follow the federal rule on prohibiting witnesses from sitting in the courtroom during the trial. However, the same rule that bans witnesses creates a special exemption for others. If the prosecutor identifies the police witness as someone he or she feels is "essential" in presenting the government's case, the judge may permit the presence of the officer at or near the prosecutor's table throughout the trial.

Prosecutors generally have an established policy regarding whether to allow a police officer, even the principal investigator in the case, to sit at counsel table during the course of the trial. Some believe it will detract from the juror's perception of the officer's objectivity. Notwithstanding that concern, officers who have sat at counsel table through at least one complete trial seem to have more confidence and competence as witnesses in their future cases. The police witness is well-served by knowing how the rule operates:

Federal Rule of Evidence 615 — Exclusion of Witnesses

At the request of a party the court shall order witnesses excluded so that they cannot hear the testimony of other witnesses, and it may make the order of its own motion. This rule does not authorize exclusion of (1) a party who is a natural person, or (2) an officer or employee of a party which is not a natural person designated as its representative by its attorney, or (3) a person whose presence is shown by a party to be essential to the presentation of the party's cause, or (4) a person authorized by statute to be present.

§ 2-4(j). Witness Checklist.

(1) Allow yourself one and one-half the amount of time you think you will need to get to the courthouse; be sure you have your subpoena; and upon arrival check in with the prosecuting attorney's office.

(2) Your appearance for court should be neat and well groomed. Wear only necessary jewelry (wedding and engagement rings) or very simple and understated jewelry and no perfume or cologne. Your clothing should reflect your occupation and your respect for the court. As a uniformed police officer, it is appropriate to appear in court in uniform. Police officers should consult with the prosecutor's office to determine whether they are permitted to wear their weapon in the courtroom.

(3) Be serious, polite and respectful in your demeanor at all times. Conduct yourself in this reserved and courteous manner whenever you are in and around the courthouse or in any public place you may be prior to a verdict being reached in the case. Jurors may be anywhere. Do not smoke, talk loudly, laugh, or discuss your testimony with anyone outside of the courtroom.

(4) Take the witness chair with no expectation that you will ever be leaving it. You are done when you are done. As soon as your thoughts become focused on getting off the stand, you increase the chance that you will give an answer that will extend your testimony.

(5) *Important.* You control whether the judge or jury hears the truth. Each question you answer requires you to review the picture in your "mind's eye" of what you saw, did or knew at a specific moment in time. "Truth" is simply the sincere effort to describe reality. You stay "truthful" so long as the testimony you give accurately describes your visual picture of reality. The most experi-

enced attorney, with all of the logic in the world is not capable of confusing or misguiding you, as long as your testimony is consistent with your mental picture.

(6) Use words within the comfort range of your vocabulary and comprehensible to an audience of sixth graders. Testimony that signals to the jury that the witness has taken time to clarify terms-of-art or vocabulary with which lay people may not be familiar puts the officer and the jurors on the same level and demonstrates the witness' consideration for the juror's lack of specific knowledge.

(7) Some attorneys may seem like they want to hurry you along in your testimony. It may be that the attorney is nervous or has seen witnesses become confused and lose their composure. You never need to worry about time; you control the tempo of the questioning. No one can proceed until you have completed your answer. But don't use your control over time just to annoy the attorney. Find the tempo that suits you for answering questions.

(8) You should never have any reason to show your temper. When you do not completely understand or hear a particular question, say so. If the question is partly true and partly untrue, you may have to let everyone know there's a problem. You should do that by saying: "May I explain?" If for some reason you aren't allowed an opportunity to immediately explain an answer, be patient, the prosecutor heard your request and, unless there are strong reasons against it, you will be allowed to give a full explanation during redirect examination.

(9) Listen closely to the question. If you do not possess the knowledge necessary to answer a question, the truthful answer is "I Don't Know." If you are sure that you once possessed the knowledge, but you can't recall, then the truthful answer is "I Don't Recall."

(10) A List of Things Witnesses Should Not Do:

<u>DO NOT</u>:

- try to answer a question unless you understand every part of it;
- give an affirmative answer to any question unless you agree with every part of it;
- volunteer information;
- guess;
- exaggerate;
- use police jargon;
- nullify information you are certain about by adding words like: "I think" or "I believe";
- answer questions with just a head nod or an "uh, huh";
- try to outsmart the defense attorney;
- analyze whether your answer is helping or hurting a particular side;

- try to resist or avoid answering a question when you know the answer;
- look at the prosecutor when you are answering questions for the defense attorney;
- display any anger or hostility or impatience;
- interrupt anyone, attorneys, judge, or court reporter, when they are talking;
- hesitate to admit the fact that you and the prosecutor met and discussed your testimony. If you are invited to explain what instructions you were given, you were instructed: "to always tell the truth, and to let the chips fall where they may";
- agree to perform any calculations or interpret the meaning of any document from the witness stand if complying with the request would require the jury to sit in a silent courtroom for more than a minute. It is better to ask if you could do it during a recess (when you are less nervous about making the jury wait for you); and
- continue speaking when you hear one of the attorneys voice an objection. The objection is almost always about a question and rarely about anything you have done. If the Judge "sustains" the objection the attorney questioning you will ask you a new question; if the Judge "overrules" the objection, you will be permitted to answer the original question. If you don't recall exactly what the original question was (that often happens when an objection interrupts your train of thought), just ask the court reporter to repeat it for you.

(11) The ten objections you are most likely to hear include:

- The question is leading the witness;
- The question asks the witness to speculate and improperly express an opinion instead of state a fact;
- The question repeats an earlier question by the prosecutor to the witness;
- The question is confusing and unintelligible;
- The question includes a misstatement of the evidence;
- The question includes the prosecutor's mischaracterization of the evidence;
- The question calls for hearsay;
- The response fails to answer the question posed and "volunteers" information about which the witness has not been asked;
- The witness unnecessarily injected hearsay into an answer; and
- The witness is narrating a response that is beyond the subject matter of the question.

Chapter 3

DIRECT EXAMINATION

§ 3-1. Direct Examination Testimony Must First Be Credible.
§ 3-2. Direct Examination — Goals.
§ 3-3. Direct Examination Question Strings for Traffic Officers.
§ 3-4. Elevating Quality of Police Officer's Testimony.
    § 3-4(a). Special Training and Experience.
    § 3-4(b). Measurement Accuracy and Completeness.
    § 3-4(c). Basis for Reconstruction, SFST, and DRE Methodologies.
    § 3-4(d). Certainty of Opinion Testimony.
§ 3-5. Photographic and Videotape Evidence.
    § 3-5(a). Lens.
    § 3-5(b). Full Frame.
    § 3-5(c). Including All Perspectives.
    § 3-5(d). Photograph Details.
    § 3-5(e). Using a Filter.
    § 3-5(f). Photograph Investigators.
    § 3-5(g). Photograph Log.
    § 3-5(h). Digital Photographs.
    § 3-5(i). Videotape Evidence.
§ 3-6. Picking Fruits of "Credibility Tree."
    § 3-6(a). Calibration and Accuracy of Equipment.
    § 3-6(b). Walking Scene to Look for Potentially Exculpatory Evidence.
    § 3-6(c). Documenting Witness Locations on Drawings of Scene.
    § 3-6(d). Prior Investigations Where No Charges Brought.
    § 3-6(e). Consultations With Other Departments.
    § 3-6(f). Description of Reference Point Used for Measurements.
    § 3-6(g). Additional Measurements Not Used in Analysis of Crash.
    § 3-6(h). Multiple Measurements of Evidence, With Values Most Favorable to Defendant, Used in All Calculations.
    § 3-6(i). Drawing(s) of Scene Verified by Actual Measurements.
    § 3-6(j). Going Back to Scene of Nighttime Crash During Daylight Hours.
    § 3-6(k). Use of Models to Show Jury How Crash Occurred.
    § 3-6(*l*). Inspection of Deflated Tires and Coinciding Road Evidence.
§ 3-7. Inoculation Against Defense Attacks.
    § 3-7(a). Omissions in Evidence Gathering or Documentation.
    § 3-7(b). Expert's Opinion Differs From Testimony of Civilian Witness.
    § 3-7(c). Calculations Could Not Be Corroborated.
    § 3-7(d). Reconstructionist Not Present at Scene.
    § 3-7(e). Witness a Crash Reconstructionist Not Expert in Other Areas.
    § 3-7(f). No Statement From Defendant.
    § 3-7(g). Unprepared Witness.
    § 3-7(h). No Tests Performed on Vehicles Involved in Crash.

§ 3-1. Direct Examination Testimony Must First Be Credible.

The well-structured, well-practiced, and well-executed direct examination must have as its primary goal to be an effective vehicle for establishing and promoting the police witness' credibility. Credibility is the essential ingredient of all successful police witness testimony. Until the jurors find the witness credible, the witness has nothing that he or she can contribute in the case.

Secondly, it should be an intelligent conversation between the police witness and the prosecutor about the substance of the case, the facts from which objective reality can be discerned. This conversation is conducted in the manner of an interview, for the benefit of the jury. The duty of the prosecutor as interviewer is to posit questions to the witness that "direct" the witness through his or her testimony in a clear and logical manner.

§ 3-2. Direct Examination — Goals.

Effective testimony by the police witness on direct examination accomplishes several important goals:

- establishs credibility with the jury;
- lays the legally required foundations for expressing opinions and explanations;
- presents basic testimony — by describing the witness' activities, motivations, and observations to the jury in a clear, logical, and visual manner;
- provides physical proof (real evidence) in support of testimonial evidence;
- utilizes visual aids that isolate and anchor the jurors' acceptance of information as part of the reality of the case;
- demonstrates behavior, incriminating or otherwise, that helps the jury better grasp the reality of the events in the case; and
- inoculates the witness from most, if not all, cross-examination attacks.

In Chapter 2, an overall design or structure for the direct examination was identified: Part I. Narration (testimony – without exhibits); Part II. Inoculation (insulating the police witness from anticipated defense attacks); and Part III. Exhibits (highlighting key points of the testimony using exhibits and demonstrations).

For most police witnesses, the Part I Narration stage of the direct examination will include several special categories of questions:

- Questions that elicit the police witness' professional qualifications;
- Questions establishing a witness' basis for knowing certain case facts;

- Questions that require opinion testimony; and
- Basis or rationale for the opinion(s).

§ 3-3. Direct Examination Question Strings for Traffic Officers.

Introductory questions:

Q. What is your name?

Q. What is your occupation?

Q. By whom are you employed?

Q. How long have you been employed as a police officer?

Q. Describe the extent of your formal education to the jury.

Q. Describe the extent of your formal police training to the jury.

Q. Are you a certified law enforcement officer in this state?

Foundation questions to establish credibility in DWI cases:

Q. Have you received special training in the enforcement of the DWI-related laws of this state? Describe that training.

Q. Describe the field sobriety tests you use.

Q. Are you certified to invoke the implied consent law of this state? Describe the certification process.

Q. Are you a certified operator of the (breath testing instrument)?

Q. Describe the certification process.

Q. When were you certified as an operator?

Q. Have you received special training in processing traffic crashes?

Q. Prior to this case being tried today, approximately how many DWI and DWI-related cases have you investigated?

Q. Approximately how many investigations or arrests have you been involved in where you determined that the defendant was "impaired?"

Questions concerning the "reasonable suspicion" for the vehicle stop:

Q. You are the officer who arrested the defendant for driving while under the influence of intoxicating liquor?

Q. Where were you at (time) on (date)?

Q. Were you on duty?

Q. Were you in uniform?

Q. Were you operating a marked (or unmarked) patrol car?

Q. Describe the circumstances that led up to your first contact with the defendant.

Q. What did you observe about the way the defendant's vehicle was being driven?

Q. How long did you follow it?

Q. What did you do?

Questions about initial observations of the defendant's demeanor:

Q. What did you notice when the defendant gave you his driver's license?

Q. What did you do?

Q. What observations did you make of the defendant as he got out of his car?

Q. Was there any explanation given for his blood-shot eyes/his poor balance/his rumpled clothing/his slurred speech/his flushed complexion?

Questions concerning field sobriety tests:

Q. What field sobriety tests did you ask the defendant to perform?

Q. Did the defendant agree to perform the tests?

Q. Describe the location where the tests were performed.

Q. What were the weather conditions at that time?

Q. Which test did he do first?

Q. What instructions did you give him on that test?

Q. Was the test demonstrated for the defendant?

Q. Describe the results of the defendant's performance on that test.

Q. How did you record the results of that test?

Q. Was the defendant allowed to retake the test? If so, with what result?

(The appropriate questions above can be repeated for each field sobriety test).

Questions to eliminate defendant's excuses for failing any of the field sobriety tests:

Q. Were there any claims, at that time or anytime since, that the defendant was taking any medications that affected his performance on these field sobriety tests?

Q. Were there any claims, at that time or anytime since, that the defendant was ill or was injured in any manner that affected his performance on these field sobriety tests?

Q. Describe the defendant's speech and behavior during this time.

Questions regarding implied consent:

Q. Was implied consent invoked in this case?

Q. What specimen was obtained from the defendant?

Q. Was the sample obtained with the consent of the defendant?

Q. What type of breath testing instrument was used in this case?

Q. Was it certified?

Q. Was the protocol followed for analyzing the defendant's breath, to ensure that the instrument was operating accurately?

Q. How is the protocol documented?

Q. What was the result of the test?

Q. How was that statement documented?

Opinion questions regarding defendant's state of intoxication or impairment:

Q. Were you able to form an opinion, based on your education, training, and ___ years of experience that includes more than _____ arrests for public intoxication or impaired driving, whether the defendant was impaired?

Q. What is that opinion?

Q. Upon what do you base your opinion?

Questions concerning statements made by the defendant:

Q. When were the defendant's Miranda Rights read to the defendant?

Q. How were they read to him?

Q. How was that documented?

Q. Why were they not read to the defendant until that point in time?

Q. Had the defendant made any statements to you before his rights were read?

Q. What statements did the defendant make to you?

Q. Did the defendant make any statements to you after his rights were read?

Q. What were these statements?

Q. How were the statements by the defendant recorded?

Questions about the search of the defendant's vehicle:

Q. Was the defendant's vehicle searched?

Q. Was the search done with a search warrant or without one?

Q. (If applicable) Who issued the search warrant?

Q. Where was the search conducted?

Q. Who conducted the search?

Q. What was found?

Q. How was it documented?

Q. Who has custody?

Questions regarding the police officer's technical investigator credentials:

Q. You were the technical investigator in this case?

Q. Describe the responsibilities of a technical investigator.

Q. Describe the education and training that went into your becoming a technical investigator.

Q. How many cases have you investigated in your capacity as a technical investigator?

Q. Describe the overall perspective of the crash scene in this case.

Q. How was that documented?

Q. What evidence was gathered at the crash scene in this case?

Q. How was the evidence and the evidence gathering process documented?

Q. Who has custody of the seized property?

Questions regarding obtaining evidence from a defendant at the hospital:

Q. Why had you gone to the hospital?

Q. How did you determine that it was safe for you to contact the defendant?

Q. Where did you speak to the defendant?

Q. Were the defendant's Miranda Rights read at that time?

Q. Why not?

Q. Did the defendant speak with you?

Q. Describe the defendant's statements to you.

Q. How were the defendant's statements documented?

Q. Was a sample of the defendant's blood obtained at the hospital?

Q. Describe the procedure that was followed for obtaining the defendant's blood sample.

Q. How was the integrity of the sample preserved?

Q. Who took custody of the sample?

Q. How long was it in your custody?

Q. What did you do with the sample? (For example, the officer delivered it to a crime lab for testing.)

Q. While in your custody were either the packaging or the seals disturbed in any manner?

Questions concerning the officer as DRE (Drug Recognition Expert):

Q. What is a drug recognition expert?

Q. Describe your education and training to become a drug recognition expert.

Q. Are you certified? By whom?

Q. Have you brought a copy of your certification with you today?

Q. How long have you been a certified drug recognition expert?

Q. Have you previously been qualified to testify as a drug recognition expert in the courts of this state?

Q. What was your involvement in the investigation of this case?

Q. Generally speaking, what is a drug influence examination?

Q. Specifically, what is involved in a drug influence examination?

Q. What are the twelve steps of the drug influence examination?

A. 1. Breath alcohol test.

2. Interview by the arresting officer.

3. Preliminary examination (includes the first of three pulses).

4. An examination of the subject's eyes.

5. Field sobriety tests, psycho-physical evaluation of the subject.

6. Examination of the subject's vital signs (includes taking the second pulse).

7. Darkroom examination of pupil size (includes an examination of the nasal and oral cavities). Locating drug administration sites on the subject's face and neck.

8. Check for muscle rigidity.

9. Check for injection sites and third pulse.

10. Interrogation, statements, and other observations.

11. Opinion of evaluator.

12. Toxicological examination (includes obtaining a urine sample from the subject).

Q. How many categories or groups of drugs can be identified through this examination?

Q. What is the basis for these groupings or categories of drugs?

Q. What are the seven groups?

Q. Upon how many people have you conducted drug influence examinations?

Q. Did you perform a drug influence examination on the defendant in this case?

Q. Please identify the defendant for the record.

Q. Were all components of the examination completed with this defendant?

Let's proceed in order through each component of the drug influence examination you conducted on the defendant:

1. Breath alcohol test:

   Q. Describe the first component, the breath-alcohol test.

   Q. What were the results?

   Q. Based on your training, education, and experience, what did this result indicate to you?

2. Interview of the arresting officer:

   Q. Regarding the second component, the jury has already heard the testimony of the arresting officer _____, so I only will ask you whether you conducted the interview of the arresting officer concerning his observations of the defendant as part of the drug influence examination?

3. Preliminary questioning and examination of the subject (including first of three pulses):

   Q. How was the questioning conducted?

   Q. Did you record the defendant's responses on the standardized drug evaluation form?

   Q. Have you brought that form with you today?

   Q. What observations did you make of the defendant as he answered the questions?

4. An examination of the subject's eyes:

   Q. Describe the parts of the eye examination.

   Q. How is the "equal tracking" part of the exam conducted?

   Q. What did you observe about the ability of the defendant's eyes to track equally?

   Q. With regard to the next part of the examination, what is a horizontal gaze nystagmus?

   Q. Describe the Horizontal Gaze Nystagmus test.

Q. Are you certified to conduct that test?

Q. Have you brought a copy of your certification with you today?

Q. Describe the first of three parts of the Horizontal Gaze Nystagmus test, the smooth pursuit.

Q. What observations did you make of the defendant's left eye?

Q. What observations did you make of the defendant's right eye?

Q. Describe the second of the three parts of the Horizontal Gaze Nystagmus test, the maximum deviation.

Q. What observations did you make of the defendant's left eye?

Q. What observations did you make of the defendant's right eye?

Q. Describe the last of the three parts of the Horizontal Gaze Nystagmus test, the onset of jerking.

Q. What observations did you make of the defendant's left eye?

Q. What observations did you make of the defendant's right eye?

Q. With regard to the next part of the examination of the defendant's eyes, what is a vertical gaze nystagmus?

Q. Describe the Vertical Gaze Nystagmus test.

Q. What observations did you make of the defendant's eyes?

Q. Describe the next part of the examination of the defendant's eyes, the eye convergence.

Q. What were the results?

Q. Describe the part of the examination regarding the defendant's pupil size.

Q. How are you able to measure pupil size?

Q. What were the results of that test?

Q. Describe how you conduct the different parts of the examination regarding the defendant's pupil reaction.

Q. What were the results of the "room light" portion of the test?

Q. What were the results of the "near total dark" portion of the test?

Q. What were the results of the "indirect light" portion of the test?

Q. What were the results of the "direct light" portion of the test?

§ 3-3   DIRECT EXAMINATION   § 3-3

5. Field sobriety tests of the subject:

    Q. In addition to your drug recognition training, what training have you received in the administration of field sobriety tests?

    Q   How many parts does the psycho-physical evaluation component of the evaluation have? How many field sobriety tests did you request that the defendant conduct?

    Q. Did the defendant attempt to perform each of these tests?

    Q. How were each of the tests explained to the defendant?

    Q. Describe (and demonstrate) the first of the four psycho-physical tests, the Rhomberg Balance Test.

    Q. What indications did the defendant give that he understood this test?

    Q. What is the purpose of this test?

    Q. What were the results of the defendant's attempt to perform this test?

    Q. Describe (and demonstrate) the second of the four tests, the walk and turn test.

    Q. What indications did the defendant give you that he understood this test?

    Q. What is the purpose of this test?

    Q. What were the results of the defendant's attempt to perform this test?

    Q. Describe (and demonstrate) the third of the four tests, the one leg stand test.

    Q. What indications did the defendant give you that he understood this test?

    Q. What is the purpose of this test?

    Q. What were the results of the defendant's attempt to perform this test?

    Q. Describe (and demonstrate) the last of the four tests, the finger to nose test.

    Q. What indications did the defendant give you that he understood this test?

    Q. What is the purpose of this test?

    Q. What were the results of the defendant's attempt to perform this test?

6. Examination of the subject's vital signs (including second of three pulses):

   Q. With regard to the component of the drug influence examination relating to obtaining the defendant's vital signs, who took the defendant's vital signs?

   Q. What specific vital signs did you take?

   Q. Describe how you measured the defendant's pulse rate.

   Q. What was the defendant's pulse rate?

   Q. When you say you are taking the defendant's blood pressure, what are you measuring?

   Q. Have you had any training in the use of instruments for measuring blood pressure?

   Q. Describe how the sphygmomanometer is used.

   Q. What was the defendant's blood pressure?

   Q. Describe how you took the defendant's temperature.

   Q. What was his temperature?

7. Dark room examinations and ingestion examination:

   Q. Describe how each step of the dark room and ingestion examinations are performed.

   Q. What observations did you make at each step?

8. Check for muscle rigidity:

   Q. Describe how you examined the defendant's muscle rigidity.

   Q. What were your observations?

9. Check for injection sites (including taking third pulse):

   Q. What does the term "drug injection administration site" refer to?

   Q. How do you conduct the component of the drug influence examination regarding drug injection administration sites?

   Q. Do you use any instruments in identifying a drug injection administration site?

   Q. What observations did you make of the defendant (his nose, mouth, arms, and neck)?

10. Interrogation, statements, and other observations:

Q. During the course of the drug influence evaluation did you speak with the defendant?

Q. What did the defendant say to you?

11. Opinions of the evaluator:

Q. Based on your observations and examination of the defendant, were you able to form an opinion as to whether the defendant was under the influence of alcohol or drugs?

Q. What is your opinion?

Q. Upon what do you base your opinion?

Q. Based on your observations and examination of the defendant, were you able to form an opinion of what type of drug was influencing the defendant?

Q. What is your opinion?

Q. Upon what do you base your opinion?

Q. Based on your observations and examination of the defendant, were you able to form an opinion as to whether the defendant was capable of safely operating a motor vehicle on that day and at that time?

Q. What is your opinion?

Q. Upon what do you base your opinion?

12. Toxicological examination:

Q. What was the final step in the twelve step drug influence examination of the defendant?

Q. Was a sample of the defendant's urine obtained?

Q. What is the purpose of obtaining a urine sample?

Q. What steps are taken prior to submission to a lab to ensure the integrity of the sample?

Q. Do you know what the results were of the toxicological examination?

Opinions and conclusion:

Q. Based on your training and experience, observations and examination of the defendant, and results of the toxicological examination, were you able to form an opinion of what type of drug was influencing the defendant?

Q. What is your opinion?

Q. Upon what do you base your opinion?

Q. Based on your training and experience, observations and examination of the defendant, and the results of the toxicological examination, were you able to form an opinion as to whether the defendant was capable of safely operating a motor vehicle on that day and at that time?

Q. What is your opinion?

Q. Upon what do you base your opinion?

Questions regarding police officer as an accident reconstructionist:

Q. You are an accident reconstructionist?

Q. What does an accident reconstructionist do?

Q. What special education or training have you obtained in the field of accident reconstruction?

Q. Have you ever taught the classes or courses in accident reconstruction? Explain.

Q. With what professional associations are you affiliated?

Q. Have you testified in court proceedings as an expert in accident reconstruction?

Q. Approximately how many accident reconstructions have you performed?

Questions concerning the principles and methodologies of accident reconstruction:

Q. Explain the basic science involved with reconstructing crashes.

Q. Explain the following vocabulary terms: (list terms).

Q. What special instruments or pieces of equipment are used in conducting an accident reconstruction?

Questions about activities of the police officer-accident reconstructionist in the present case:

Q. How did you become involved in this case?

Q. Describe your specific activities in this case.

Q. What materials have you examined?

Q. Who have you spoken to about this case?

Q. Were you able to form an opinion of (state the relevant subject of the opinion: speed, point of impact, visibility, etc.) based on a reasonable degree of scientific certainty?

Q. What is that opinion?

Q. Upon what do you base that opinion?

§ 3-4. Elevating Quality of Police Officer's Testimony.

The authors endorse the concept that a successful direct examination is structured so that as much as 90% of the testimony focuses on establishing a personal, professional, and legal foundation for the jury's acceptance of the witness' testimonial evidence.

§ 3-4(a). Special Training and Experience.

The prosecutor and police witness are asking the jurors to believe the officer's testimonial representations regarding the culpability of the defendant. Ultimately the defense will attack the competency of the police, highlighting alleged shortcomings in the officer's credentials, incompleteness in the investigation, or prosecution bias. All jury verdicts come down to "who to believe?"

The most valuable tool the witness has is credibility, and the basis for that credibility logically starts with the witness' training and experience. But all too often the qualifying questions bring out what sounds like the ordinary level of training that any police officer would have instead of stressing special training and experience in the witness' background.

The qualifying questions should be constructed in much the same manner as a professional resume, emphasizing and distinguishing the witness' credentials as they relate to the particular type of case being prosecuted. Whenever possible, the qualifying questions should distinguish the witness from other officers in his/her department.

In this regard, the officer's qualifying testimony might include:

(1) Number of crashes investigated (including the number in which the officer was the chief investigator): If the officer is called into an investigation because of his/her expertise, this should always be explained to the jury. A mention of cases in which the officer was in charge of the investigation and a short descrip-

tion of the distinction of being the chief investigator can help the jury understand the special abilities of the witness.

(2) Number of crashes of this specific type (pedestrian, motorcycle, etc.) in which the officer was an investigator or reconstructionist: Mentioning the fact that the officer has worked on numerous similar crashes, and pointing out investigative activities specific to the type of crash in question, may help persuade the jury.

(3) Describing special training in terms of who offered the training, where the training was given, who instructed the training (including his/her credentials), the length of the training, whether the number of participants was restricted, how participants were evaluated, etc. This information can distinguish the training from "ordinary training that is part of the regular education of all officers."

SAMPLE TESTIMONY: Explain to the jury that the officer has taken a special course on crash investigation.

> Q. Officer, have you had any special training?
>
> A. Yes, two years ago I took a forty-hour course that the State Patrol offered.
>
> Q. Was that in addition to your ordinary academy training as a recruit officer?
>
> A. Yes it was.

BETTER TESTIMONY:

> Q. Officer, have you had any special training in crash investigation?
>
> A. Yes, two years ago I took a forty-hour course offered by the State Patrol.
>
> Q. How many officers were in that course?
>
> A. Just 35 officers took the course.
>
> Q. And how many officers from your own department received that special training?
>
> A. I was the only one.
>
> Q. Did you receive any certification as a result of that training?
>
> A. Yes, after taking a final exam, I was certified in Advanced Crash Investigation.
>
> Q. How many officers in your own department are certified at that level?

A. There are only three of us that have that certification.

Q. And how many officers are in your department?

A. Sixty-eight.

Any in-service seminars attended by the officer might be brought to the attention of the jurors, pointing out recognized speakers or instructors, as well as any memberships in professional associations or organizations relating to the expertise of the witness.

(4) High-profile or unusual cases that demonstrate the officer's special abilities: If the officer participated in a case that received media attention or involved people recognized in the community, it may portray the officer's special abilities or expertise. Reference to such a case gives the witness an opportunity to "tell a story" to the jurors and establish a communication tone that is casual and free-flowing. As such, it may break the ice with one or more jurors and open the door to more attentive listening for the rest of the testimony.

(5) Appointment as an instructor or presentations as a speaker at a conference or meeting: The fact that a witness has been an instructor of other officers immediately elevates the witness in the eyes of the jury. The trust that others have placed in the witness by accepting him/her as an instructor inherently carries with it a recognition of the witness' abilities.

(6) Participation in the investigations of other neighboring departments that establish the officer's role as a consultant: Sometimes several departments form an informal consortium or network of reconstructionists, DRE's, Intoxilyzer operators, etc. who regularly communicate about their particular fields of expertise. If the witness is part of such a network it should be pointed out to the jurors, as it helps to establish that others recognize the officer as competent in the field.

SAMPLE TESTIMONY: Regarding the witness' consulting with other departments on their cases:

Q. Officer, have you had occasion to assist other police departments in any cases?

A. Yes, several officers from other departments and myself discuss our cases.

Q. Why do you do that?

A. Because one of us may have an idea or a different way of looking at the evidence that is helpful.

Q. Approximately how often do you do this sort of thing?

A. Oh, maybe once a month or so.

BETTER TESTIMONY:

Q. Officer, have you ever been asked by another police department to assist them in analyzing a crash?

A. Yes, I've been contacted by other departments to consult on particular crashes and to assist in the reconstruction.

Q. How does such contact usually originate?

A. There are a number of us who communicate informally on a regular basis about new ideas in reconstruction, new equipment that's out, and that sort of thing. It's a way of keeping up to date. And in some cases we call each other and discuss the facts of a case to see if there might be something else we could do.

Q. How many times have you been asked by another department to help with one of their cases?

A. Probably a dozen times, or so.

Q. Do you ever consult with another officer on one of your cases?

A. Sometimes, if there is some uncertainty in the interpretation of the evidence or the use of a particular method of reconstructing the crash.

Q. Did you consult with anyone on this case?

A. No.

Since the officer best knows any such background that would fortify the qualifications testimony, it is appropriate for the officer to prepare his/her own qualifying questions and to give them to the prosecutor with whom he/she works. The credibility and professional career of the officer are at stake, and the prosecutor would welcome this assistance. After all, the goal of the prosecutor/witness team is to establish the credibility of the police officer and to persuade the jury to accept the officer's opinion(s). While it may be impractical for the prosecutor to sit down with each individual police witness and carefully construct qualifying questions for each one, the officer can and should.

Trial Tip

It is helpful to customize the qualifying questions to the specific case being tried.

---

§ 3-4(b). Measurement Accuracy and Completeness.

The police witness' credibility can be greatly enhanced by testimony that demonstrates that his/her measurements made at the scene were done in a professional, complete, and accurate way. Since this testimony involves fact evidence, it is only minimally cross-examinable, but it helps the witness connect with the jurors and establish a tone for the opinion testimony that will follow.

It is helpful to establish that the police investigator is well-trained, and that the investigation has been conducted according to established policies. Some examples of this type of testimony include:

(1) *Description of equipment used to make measurements.* Both the crash investigator and the prosecutor may be thoroughly familiar with the measurements and measuring equipment that was used to document the physical evidence at the scene. But jurors may be less knowledgeable about a particular piece of equipment and will appreciate an officer who clarifies what the equipment is used for, the manner in which it is used, its intrinsic degree of accuracy, etc. If a juror misunderstands a piece of equipment, it opens the door for a misrepresentation or suggestion of inaccuracy during the cross-examination. And, since the measurements may be the input to the crash reconstructionist's calculations, a misunderstanding may affect the credibility of the opinion in the juror's mind. A few minutes taken to clarify such a point shows a courtesy toward the jurors that makes the officer more likable; and don't overlook the value it may have in educating the judge as well. In this regard, the credibility of the police witness may bear heavily on the limits a judge places on the officer's opinion testimony. Examples might include the use of a drag sled, use of an accelerometer to measure road friction, the use of a rolling wheel to make distance measurements, employing an electronic instrument to make a forensic mapping of a crash scene and produce a detailed scale drawing, etc.

SAMPLE TESTIMONY: Explaining how a "rolling wheel" is used to make distance measurements at the scene.

    Q. Officer, did you measure the skid marks?

    A. Yes, I measured the marks with a rolling wheel.

    Q. Is that a piece of equipment that you ordinarily use when you investigate a crash?

    A. Yes, I've used it many times in the past.

    Q. Can you tell the jury what you found?

BETTER TESTIMONY:

Q. Officer, did you measure the skid marks?

A. Yes.

Q. How did you measure the skid marks?

A. I measured the marks with a rolling wheel.

Q. Would you tell the jury what a rolling wheel is?

A. It's a wheel with a handle on it, and the wheel is connected by gears to a counter so that when you roll the wheel, the counter indicates the distance you have moved the wheel. It's like the ones you sometimes see road construction people using to measure distances.

Q. Is that a piece of equipment that you ordinarily use when you investigate a crash?

A. Yes, I carry one in my car and I've used it many times in the past.

Q. Can you tell the jury what measurements you made?

These few extra sentences of testimony paint a clearer picture of the measuring equipment and helps the officer connect with the jurors by demonstrating his willingness to clarify a term-of-art that might be misunderstood by one of the jurors.

Trial Tip

Don't underestimate the value of a few minutes spent on an explanation; jurors will appreciate the effort and consideration.

---

(2) *Accuracy of measurements made at the scene.* This testimony includes, but is not limited to, the accuracy of the measurements and the calibration of the measuring instrument(s) against a known standard. The investigator often takes for granted that the measuring equipment is accurate, but the defense cross-examination often attempts to infer otherwise, since the measurements are the basis for the reconstruction calculations. Talking about accuracy and the certainty of measurements during the direct examination usually prevents lengthy cross-examination on the topic, and at the same time shows the jury that the officer recognizes the importance of assuring accuracy in his/her measurements.

SAMPLE TESTIMONY: The accuracy of the rolling wheel used to make distance measurements.

    Q. Is the rolling wheel a piece of equipment that you ordinarily use to make distance measurements?

    A. Yes, I've used it many times.

    Q. How accurate is it?

    A. It measures to a tenth of a foot accuracy.

BETTER TESTIMONY:

    Q. Is the rolling wheel a piece of equipment that you ordinarily use to make distance measurements?

    A. Yes, every cruiser is equipped with a wheel.

    Q. How accurate are the measurements made with the rolling wheel?

    A. It reads to a tenth of a foot accuracy.

    Q. How do you know the measuring wheel is accurate when you are using it?

    A. I stretch out a 100-foot tape measure and roll my wheel over it to make sure it reads 100, then after my measurements are finished I do it again to be sure the wheel was accurate.

    Q. And did you check that it was accurate when you used it in this case?

    A. Yes.

Again, a few extra lines of testimony may add credibility to later opinion testimony by the same officer, or even another witness in the state's case.

    (3) *Completeness of the measurements and investigation.* Jurors often feel that an officer is more credible if he/she has made multiple measurements, documented the manner in which the measurements were made, or demonstrates that the measurements were consistent with standard departmental policy. The question, "And is that standard departmental policy?" goes a long way toward establishing fairness and a lack of bias in the investigation. It also raises the police investigator above the muck of questions that would infer an incompleteness or lack of professionalism in the investigation. When the facts of the case would clearly prove the culpability of the defendant, one of the few viable defense tactics is to attack the investigation itself and to cast a doubt on the accuracy of the evidence. Remember, the credibility of the investigation is the

foundation for much of the other opinion testimony that addresses the ultimate legal issue(s) in the case.

By doing multiple measurements the officer takes into account any slight variations in the evidence (e.g., slight drag factor differences at various points along the skid mark pattern), and assures the jury that any possible measurement errors were avoided. By documenting the way the measurement was made either photographically or in writing, who witnessed or assisted with the measurement, the specific conditions of the measurement, etc. the witness establishes additional credibility. Of course, the strength of such testimony depends on the officer's awareness at the scene that the investigation is directly related to the officer's credibility at trial.

SAMPLE TESTIMONY: Regarding multiple measurements of the drag factor over the 200-foot skid mark pattern.

Q. Did you make more than one measurement of the drag factor?

A. Yes, I measured it at the beginning, in the middle, and at the end of the skid pattern.

Q. Why did you do that?

A. To make sure that there wasn't any significant difference in the drag factor along the length of the skid pattern.

BETTER TESTIMONY:

Q. Did you make multiple measurements of the drag factor of the road?

A. Yes.

Q. Can you tell the jury how and why you made more than one measurement?

A. The skid pattern was about 200 feet long, so I measured the drag factor every twenty feet along the skid marks. A road surface usually doesn't vary significantly in such a short distance, and by making measurements close together I was able to confirm that the road was consistent in this case.

Q. Did the measurements made every twenty feet differ at all?

A. Yes. There was a slight difference only in the last decimal position, so I used the smallest measured value to give the benefit to the defendant.

Q. Is that what you ordinarily do with this type of measurement?

A. Yes. That's how I've been trained to do it, and it's our departmental policy to do it that way.

SAMPLE TESTIMONY: Regarding the description of the reference point used for the measurements.

Q. Can you describe what you did in making your measurements?

A. First, I chose a utility pole (# SP/413) as a reference point for my measurements. Then I made all my measurements North, South, East, and West of the pole, using the pole as a zero point.

BETTER TESTIMONY:

Q. Can you tell the jury what you did to make your measurements at the scene?

A. First, I selected a permanent point, the South edge of utility pole # SP/413 as a zero point for all my measurements. That established a North-South, East-West grid for all my measurements.

Q. Why did you select a utility pole as your reference point?

A. The reference point has to be permanent, and the city has a record of its location on the site maps in the City Engineer's office.

Q. Why did you use the South edge of the pole as your reference point?

A. So I would actually have a single point where I could place the end of my tape measure for the measurements.

Here is an example of testimony that shows a sense of the completeness and the lack of bias in the officer's investigation while processing the scene:

Q. Officer, what else did you do while you were processing the scene?

A. I walked several hundred feet back from the point of impact and looked for road defects.

Q. Can you tell the jury what you mean by road defects?

A. Yes. I was looking for potholes or irregularities in the road surface or along the edge of the road that might have been a factor in the way the defendant's vehicle behaved just before the collision — which might have caused the defendant to lose control of the vehicle.

Q. And do you usually do that as part of your investigation?

A. In cases where loss of control or an unusual pre-impact motion of a vehicle is involved I do, yes.

Q. Did you find any road defects or condition which would have caused the defendant's vehicle to go out of control?

A. No, I didn't find anything of that sort.

In summary, here are some ways to establish credibility while offering testimony about measurements made at the scene:

- describe calibration against a known standard;
- make multiple measurements to avoid errors;
- give the benefit of any measurement differences to the defendant;
- have someone else observe the measurements being made;
- photograph the measurements being made;
- describe the limitations and accuracy of the measurements;
- document the measurement conditions, witnesses, etc.;
- describe other measurements that were not used in the calculations or in reaching opinions; and
- establish that all measurements were made according to departmental policy and consistent with prior training.

§ 3-4(c). Basis for Reconstruction, SFST, and DRE Methodologies.

The jury needs to know that there is a scientific basis for the opinion testimony that an officer may provide. In the case of crash reconstruction, they need to understand that principles of physics are applied to crashes to determine vehicle speeds, directions of travel, time-distance relationships, etc. A general discussion is usually helpful and can make some jurors feel comfortable and intuitively satisfied with opinion testimony even though they may not fully understand exactly how the opinion was reached mathematically. This need must be balanced against the possibility that such testimony will alienate a jury who feels the witness is "talking over their head," so the testimony must be at a layman's level with a minimum of technical terminology.

The reconstruction witness should be prepared to cite field studies or staged tests that validate the methods used to reach the ultimate opinion. Personal participation in such tests should be presented, and the widespread acceptance of the equations should be made clear to the jury and to the judge. The fact should be made clear that the methodologies used in a particular case are part of standardized training, are cited in published texts, and are written about in journals.

DIRECT EXAMINATION

§ 3-4(c)

SAMPLE TESTIMONY: On the use of the minimum speed from skid marks equation to estimate vehicle speed.

Q. Officer, can you describe to the jury how you estimated the speed of the defendant's vehicle in this case?

A. I used an equation called the "minimum speed from skid marks" equation.

Q. Was that equation taught to you at the police academy?

A. Yes.

Q. And is it widely accepted in the field of crash reconstruction?

A. Yes.

Q. By using that equation did you arrive at an opinion of the defendant's speed in this case?

A. Yes.

BETTER TESTIMONY:

Q. Officer, did you perform any calculations to determine the speed of the defendant's vehicle in this case?

A. Yes, I used an equation called "the minimum speed from skid marks" equation.

Q. Is that an equation that is widely accepted in the field of crash reconstruction?

A. Yes. It is published in textbooks and is one of the most fundamental equations that we use.

Q. What is the basis of the equation?

A. It is based on the fact that when the vehicle is moving it has what is called "kinetic energy." The kinetic energy is related to the speed of the vehicle and evidence of that energy is found in the length of the skid marks that the vehicle makes and the friction or "stickiness" of the road.

Q. What evidence do you need to use that equation?

A. You need to know the length of the skid marks, and also an index of the road friction called the "drag factor."

Q. Did you make measurements of that evidence as part of your investigation?

A. Yes. I personally made the measurements.

Q. As a result of your investigation were you able to use the minimum speed from skid marks equation to determine the speed of the defendant's vehicle?

A. Yes.

Similarly, the DWI and DRE officers should clarify to the jurors that the SFST's and the methodology of drug recognition are also based on scientific studies using human populations. A simple demonstration of a principle upon which a given test is based can help the witness connect with jurors, and avoid any defense claims that such tests are "voodoo science." The witness should be prepared to cite studies that support his/her opinion and methodology, when such studies are available.

NHTSA has conducted numerous studies involving hundreds of impaired drivers. Our book, *Investigation and Prosecution of DWI and Vehicular Homicide* (LEXIS® Law Publishing), cites the NHTSA June 1992 study (1), the Thair, Burns, and Moskowitz March 1981 study (2), and several other studies that validate field sobriety tests.(3,4,5) Also in that book, several studies concerning the validity of the horizontal gaze nystagmus are cited. (6,7)

Trial Tip

The fact that the methodologies and practices used by police are "widely accepted by others in the field" or are standard departmental practice goes a long way toward having the jurors (and the judge) accept the testimony.

With regard to the issue of horizontal gaze nystagmus, NHTSA has recently published an excellent research guide for judges, prosecutors and law enforcement, which was compiled by the American Prosecutors Research Institute (APRI) of the National Traffic Law Center. The guide is titled *Horizontal Gaze Nystagmus HGN: The Science and the Law*. It encompasses not only many of the scientific studies, but case law summaries, standards for admitting scientific evidence, and predicate questions for the arresting/SFST officer. For information on how to obtain the guide, contact APRI at 703-549-4253 or visit their website at www.ndaa-apri.org.

§ 3-4(d). Certainty of Opinion Testimony.

In the case of a reconstructionist, the credibility of opinion testimony can be bolstered by calculations called "sensitivity analysis," in which input values are changed to see what effect such changes have on the calculated results. Computer spread sheets such as Excel or Lotus can facilitate such analyses, with hundreds of variations of the input numbers calculated in a few seconds. The witness should do these analyses routinely to support opinions and in anticipation of defense attacks on the accuracy of field measurements.

d (ft)	f	S (mph)	K.E. (lbft)	% Deviation
140	0.700	54.22	296264	3.39
140	0.705	54.42	324881	3.05
140	0.710	54.61	327185	2.70
140	0.715	54.80	329489	2.36
140	0.720	54.99	331793	2.02
140	0.725	55.18	334097	1.68
140	0.730	55.37	336402	1.34
140	0.735	55.56	338706	1.01
140	0.740	55.75	341010	0.67
140	0.745	55.94	343314	0.33
140	0.750	56.12	345618	0.00
140	0.755	56.31	347922	0.33
140	0.760	56.50	350226	0.66
140	0.765	56.68	352530	1.00
140	0.770	56.87	354834	1.32
140	0.775	57.05	357139	1.65
140	0.780	57.24	359443	1.98
140	0.785	57.42	361747	2.31
140	0.790	57.60	364051	2.63
140	0.795	57.78	366355	2.96
140	0.800	57.97	368659	3.28

Sensitivity analysis shows that a variation in the drag factor value does not significantly affect the estimated vehicle speed.

By including the entire range of values of the physical evidence that might have resulted from measurement errors, the reconstructionist should be satisfied that his/her opinion cannot be changed significantly. This gives the witness a sense of security, and prepares the witness to handle hypothetical questions that are composed by the defense attorney. As a note, the police witness usually must answer the defense hypothetical, but should not feel helpless in doing so. The police witness should alert the jurors to the fact that the hypothetical facts do not agree with the evidence in the case.

For years the author was asked the following question: "If the measurements made by the police were wrong, then wouldn't the calculations using those measurements be wrong?" While the answer intuitively seems to be yes because different numbers put into the calculator yield different answers out of the calculator, the real question is whether such calculations are significantly different from those already offered in testimony. Recently when asked this same question, the author asked the defense attorney, "How wrong were the police measurements?" This required the defense attorney to compose a more specific hypothetical question. This posed quite a challenge for the attorney, and the jury saw through the deception of the hypothetical. The jury can be alerted to the distortion in the evidence by asking the question, "But, sir, those are not the facts in evidence in this case, are they?" This technique must be used carefully so as not to appear argumentative or provocative to the judge. If there is no foundation for the hypothetical, the prosecutor may object on the basis that the hypothetical is based on "facts not in evidence," but this may be overruled if the defense attorney suggests otherwise, or that the foundation will be forthcoming.

When a hypothetical is being constructed by the defense attorney, he/she will often use the language, "If I were to tell you.…" This suggests that what he/she is about to say is probably not a fact in evidence, but is speculation by the defense attorney in an attempt to change the witness' picture of the facts in the case. An appropriate response to such a question might be "Are you saying that … is fact in this case?" This response alerts the jurors that something is happening to distort the facts, but it should only be used in a friendly, inquisitive tone so as not to hurt the witness' credibility. Some judges may alert the witness not to talk to the defense attorney in such cases, but to answer the question as best the witness is able.

SAMPLE TESTIMONY: Where the defense attorney is trying to change the witness' testimony about the defendant's visibility distance in a rear-end collision.

Q. If it was raining the night of the crash, the visibility would have been less than you have stated in your testimony, wouldn't it?

A. Are you saying that it was raining at the time of the crash?

(In fact, it was not.)

§ 3-5. Photographic and Videotape Evidence.

Photographs vividly portray the scene of the crash, and there are a number of considerations in producing the most effective (and admissible) photographic exhibits at trial, including:

§ 3-5(a). Lens.

The camera should have a 45-50 mm lens to best capture an accurate picture of what would be seen by the human eye.

§ 3-5(b). Full Frame.

Exhibits should be printed "full frame," meaning the picture should have dimensions in a ratio of 1:1.5 since that is the size of the negative on 35 mm film. Prints made 4 x 6, 6 x 9, and 8 x 12 will satisfy this format and contain all the information from the negative. Other sized prints require the negative to be cropped and may elicit an admissibility objection from the defense.

§ 3-5(c). Including All Perspectives.

Photographs should be taken from the perspectives of all operators and witnesses to best capture the lighting, view restrictions, etc., for later use.

SAMPLE TESTIMONY: Regarding a photograph of the perspective of a civilian witness in a pedestrian crash.

> Q. Officer, I show you Exhibit #4. Do you recognize this photograph?
>
> A. Yes, I took this photograph.
>
> Q. What is depicted in this photograph?
>
> A. It shows the view that the civilian witness, Mrs. Smith, had of the crash.
>
> Q. Is it a true and accurate representation of the view from Mrs. Smith's position?
>
> A. Yes.

BETTER TESTIMONY:

> Q. Officer, I show you Exhibit #4. Do you recognize this photograph?
>
> A. Yes, I took it from the position where Mrs. Smith was standing when she observed the crash.

Q. Does it accurately depict the view that Mrs. Smith had of the crash scene?

A. Yes. I asked her where she was when she observed the crash, and then I noted it in my field notes and on my drawing of the scene.

Q. Why did you take this photograph as part of your investigation?

A. Because it shows the lighting, the foliage, and the layout of the streets, and I felt it might assist Mrs. Smith and help the jury to understand her testimony at a later time.

Q. Is it standard procedure to take this type of photograph from the witness' perspective?

A. Yes.

§ 3-5(d). Photograph Details.

Road evidence should be photographed from various angles and distances, with close-ups of tire tread patterns and other physical evidence which may prove helpful at trial.

§ 3-5(e). Using a Filter.

The use of a "polarizing filter" on the camera can reduce glare and result in much clearer photographs of tire marks, damage to vehicles, and other evidence.

§ 3-5(f). Photograph Investigators.

Photographs of the investigator(s) making measurements of physical evidence may also be helpful in educating the jury and avoiding confusion at trial.

§ 3-5(g). Photograph Log.

Keeping an accurate log of the photographs as they are taken and noting the type of film, camera make and model, etc. enhances the jury's sense of completeness in the investigation. Regarding use of the photographs at trial, the decision on which photographs to use with a particular witness should be made in consultation with that witness, as he/she has the best idea of what effect the use of a particular photograph may have and how it best fits with the testimony. In some cases, blow-ups of the photograph are useful as an aid since this allows the witness the freedom to get down from the witness stand and converse directly with the jury. In other cases, it may be more effective for an enlargement to be used so that the witness can directly engage a few jurors at a time to explain the contents of the photograph. The witness should be familiar with how the photographs will be marked as exhibits to avoid fumbling or seeming unfamiliar with the practices of the court.

§ 3-5(h). Digital Photographs.

There has recently been some discussion about the admissibility of photographs produced by digital cameras that do not have conventional film negatives as part of the print process. The concern is that digital images can be altered on a computer, thereby presenting no secure original image in evidence. Some digital cameras have a removable diskette that stores the original image, and this chip can be removed and put into evidence just like a roll of film negatives. The legal status of admissibility of digitally-recorded images is in flux at this time (Spring, 1999), but research on this topic is being done by the American Prosecutors Research Institute (703-549-4253 or www.ndaa-apri.org).

§ 3-5(i). Videotape Evidence.

Videotape evidence is handled in much the same manner as other photographic evidence, with the additional caveat that the videotape has a soundtrack. Some video cameras allow the audio recording to be switched off; utterances made by civilians or police investigators may be captured on the soundtrack and produce an admissibility problem. Some departments may establish policies regarding the limited use of videotaping as a method of documenting a crash scene. In-car video capability is commonly used in DWI prosecutions, and many departments videotape their booking procedures. But in some cases, the impaired operator may appear only minimally impaired, because motor functions may not truly show the effects of alcohol or drugs on the brain and cognitive processes. The video camera may not pick up enough detail to capture the observations an officer can make in person while observing the alleged impaired operator.

Trial Tip

If departmental policy is or has been to videotape a crash scene, it may pose a problem if videotaping was not done. If there is no such policy, it should be mentioned during direct examination that no videotaping was done in this specific case.

---

§ 3-6. Picking Fruits of "Credibility Tree."

This section contains a wealth of information about how to make a connection with the jury while testifying and increase credibility by demonstrating (1) honesty, (2) likeability, and (3) competency. These areas of testimony will be available in most cases, and are often overlooked because they are not considered vital to the ultimate opinion(s) in the case. But prosecutors and witnesses should avail themselves of these areas of testimony to build credibility, remembering the rule that effective testimony is based on credibility, not on analysis and technical testimony. To offer this testimony, in some cases the witness has to do certain things during the investigation of the crash. But if these become standard practice, the police witness will have a foundation for building juror confidence through testimony that is virtually unattackable by the defense.

Several areas of testimony for the crash reconstructionist or investigator are given on the following pages. Similar lines of testimony, often limited to a few questions, can help establish the credibility of the DWI/DUI or DRE officer. Don't overlook the value of such testimony, as it aligns the witness with the jurors and establishes a positive rapport.

§ 3-6(a). Calibration and Accuracy of Equipment.

§ 3-6(b). Walking Scene to Look for Potentially Exculpatory Evidence.

§ 3-6(c). Documenting Witness Locations on Drawings of Scene.

A single dot or small circle on a drawing to show a witness location may seem inconsequential, but it can have significant value in the case and provide a source of credibility for the police witness at trial. The reasons for indicating witness locations on a scene drawing should be obvious:

(1) The prosecutor or others should know where the witnesses were located so they can go to the scene and observe the scene from the witness' vantage point;
(2) The documentation of the witness location shows completeness of the investigation and competency of the investigator; and
(3) Documentation of the witness location prevents the defense from moving the civilian witness to another location during the testimony of the witness, and thus reducing the value or accuracy of the civilian witness' testimony and observations.

In one case a civilian witness, Mrs. West, observed a pedestrian enter the roadway and get struck by a car. The witness' view from point A was clear and unobstructed. During cross-examination the police officer was asked to indicate on his drawing where Mrs. West was located when she observed the crash, and was unable to do so with any certainty. During Mrs. West's cross-examination she was confused about her location at the scene and was convinced that she was at point B. Later in the trial, evidence was introduced showing an obstructed view at point B, which hurt Mrs. West's prior testimony.

SAMPLE TESTIMONY:

Q. Officer, what is this little circle on your drawing?

A. It is where Mrs. West was when she observed the crash.

Q. How do you know that?

A. She showed me where she was standing when I interviewed her the night of the crash, and then I measured that position using my reference point.

Q. Why did you note her position on your drawing?

A. So that everyone would know exactly where she was. By the time a case comes to trial it might be years later and the witness wouldn't be as sure of her position, so this way there would be less chance for confusion.

Q. Is this something that you usually do as a standard part of your investigation?

A. Yes, it was pointed out to me by an instructor at a training I attended, and I've been doing it ever since.

Q. Did you do anything else to document her location?

A. Yes, I took several photographs showing her perspective of the crash scene.

§ 3-6(d). Prior Investigations Where No Charges Brought.

The witness may have worked on cases prior to the time of trial in which no charges were brought, and the investigation was therefore exculpatory. This should be pointed out to show lack of bias on the part of the police witness. Such testimony shows jurors that while the police and prosecutor are working as a team in this trial, the police officer's role is to gather evidence and present the truth to the jury.

§ 3-6(e). Consultations With Other Departments.

§ 3-6(f). Description of Reference Point Used for Measurements.

§ 3-6(g). Additional Measurements Not Used in Analysis of Crash.

The witness may have made additional measurements or done additional work that was not used in the actual reconstruction of the crash. Pointing this out to the jury shows completeness and that standard investigation procedure was followed in this case. It also can be used to show that the officer anticipated potentially exculpatory areas of evidence and gathered the evidence without any bias. As such, it can go a long way toward balancing the common defense attack that "you didn't do this, and you didn't do this, and…."

SAMPLE TESTIMONY:

> Q. Officer, you have mentioned some measurements that you made and used in your reconstruction of the crash. Is there anything else that you did, or other measurements that you made, that you did not mention in your testimony?
>
> A. There were other measurements, such as the location of the fence that was damaged by the defendant's vehicle, the location of debris from the crash, and other things that I didn't use directly in my reconstruction of the crash.
>
> Q. Why did you make those additional measurements?
>
> A. It's all part of doing a complete investigation, because at the time of the investigation you don't know what might be useful later. The idea is to document as much as possible, and even then there are things we didn't document because we could go back and get them later if we needed them.
>
> Q. What would some of those things be?
>
> A. Permanent objects like trees, utility poles, etc. that we could always measure at a later date.
>
> Q. Was it necessary in this case to go back and get any additional scene information in order to complete your reconstruction of the crash?
>
> A. No it wasn't.

§ 3-6(h). Multiple Measurements of Evidence, With Values Most Favorable to Defendant, Used in All Calculations.

§ 3-6(i). Drawing(s) of Scene Verified by Actual Measurements.

Since drawings may be represented to the court as being "to-scale," the witness who prepared the drawing should explain that its accuracy has been verified by comparing the completed drawing to the actual scene. This can be done simply by taking the drawing to the scene and making several measurements to confirm that the drawing accurately represents the dimensions of the scene. While this may seem obvious to the police witness and the prosecutor, the jurors want to feel confident that the drawing truly represents the scene.

§ 3-6(j). Going Back to Scene of Nighttime Crash During Daylight Hours.

In many cases evidence is more easily observed during daylight than at night. Preserving the scene as much as possible and going back to look for evidence and make measurements during daylight hours can sometimes add valuable information to a nighttime crash investigation. One obvious advantage is photographing road evidence, but in some cases the investigator may actually see something that was not visible at night with limited lighting capabilities. Even if nothing additional was observed, it gives the jury a sense of confidence in the investigation.

SAMPLE TESTIMONY:

Q. Officer, what time did you first arrive at the scene?

A. I got there and started my investigation about 2:30 AM.

Q. When did you finish processing the scene?

A. I finished the first part of my investigation and left the scene at about 5:00 AM that morning.

Q. Did you do anything else as part of your investigation?

A. Yes, I went back to the scene at about 6:30, after sunrise, to complete my investigation of the scene.

Q. Why did you wait until daylight to resume your investigation?

A. Because sometimes there is evidence that is better observed during the daytime, and additional photographs can be taken.

Q. Was the scene secured from 5:00 to 6:30 AM.?

A. Yes, Officer Davis stayed at the scene and routed traffic around the crash area.

Q. Did you make any additional observations when you visited the scene at 6:30 that morning?

A. Well, not really. But the tire marks and some of the other evidence was clearer, and I took additional photographs.

Q. Did you make any additional measurements at that time?

A. No. The measurements I made the previous night were all I needed.

§ 3-6(k). Use of Models to Show Jury How Crash Occurred.

The use of a scale drawing, on a horizontal surface in front of the jury, with model vehicles to the same scale, is an effective way to explain the approach, engagement, and separation. This should be done even if these facts are not disputed by defense, as it gives the officer an opportunity to get out of the witness box and connect with the jurors. A narrative might also include specific damage features that match up with vehicle motions, occupant kinematics during engagement, etc. The scene drawing itself can be discussed first, and then models can be used to demonstrate the crash to the jury.

This method is sometimes more engaging for the jurors since it occurs in a horizontal plane and is more realistic than a demonstration using a drawing on an easel. Cross-examination of this testimony affords the officer a second chance to "tell the story," to the benefit of the prosecution's case.

§ 3-6(*l*). Inspection of Deflated Tires and Coinciding Road Evidence.

In many crashes, one or more tires are suddenly deflated during impact, and the tire condition is usually noted in the investigation report. But in some cases, the sudden deflation of the tire may be offered by the defense as a cause of the erratic motion of the defendant's vehicle. The investigating officer can demonstrate his/her completeness by telling the jurors about the deflated tire(s), and evidence of when the deflation occurred, to add to the "picture" the jury will have of the crash. At the same time, such testimony will build credibility for the investigating officer or reconstructionist.

SAMPLE TESTIMONY:

> Q. Officer, did you inspect the tires on the defendant's vehicle as part of your investigation of this crash?
>
> A. Yes.
>
> Q. Can you tell the jury what you observed?
>
> A. The right front tire had been severely damaged by the impact, and was deflated. The quarter panel had been bent into the tire and caused a cut about four inches in length. In addition, the tire itself was wedged against the bent metal so it would not turn.
>
> Q. Is it standard policy to inspect and note the condition of the tires on the vehicles involved in a crash?
>
> A. Yes.
>
> Q. Why do you do that?

A. Because it is important to note any damage to the tires as it might affect steering, braking, etc. And I'm looking to see whether the flat tire might have occurred before the impact and been a cause of the erratic motion of the defendant's vehicle. The damage in this case, though, was caused by the impact itself.

Q. Did you make any other observations that would support the conclusion that the tire was damaged by the impact?

A. Yes.

Q. What observations did you make?

A. The mark on the road from the flattened tire, which we call a "scallop" mark, started at the point of impact and led away from the impact. This indicated that the tire was inflated up to the point of impact and that the crash itself had deflated the tire.

Q. Did you photograph the tire mark that you are referring to?

A. Yes.

§ 3-7. Inoculation Against Defense Attacks.

In an earlier chapter, inoculation was mentioned in the context of the structure of the direct examination. In this chapter, inoculation against cross-examination attacks will be discussed more completely since it greatly affects the ability of the police witness to maintain his/her credibility. In every investigation there are always things that may not have been done or even evidence that was not gathered, for many reasons — sometimes because the investigator made a conscious decision that it was not relevant to the case. The concept of a "complete report" depends upon the definition of "complete," because there are always observations and other information that are not memorialized in the final written report. A common defense tactic is to point out to the jury the number of things that were not done as part of the investigation in order to portray the investigator as ineffective, sloppy, and incompetent. In anticipation of such attacks the witness and prosecutor should discuss how the witness can be inoculated against such attacks in the officer's direct examination. It is during the direct examination that the prosecutor can introduce testimony that might otherwise be characterized unfairly by the defense attorney in the cross-examination. Some of the areas of inoculation follow.

§ 3-7(a). Omissions in Evidence Gathering or Documentation.

This often occurs because the significance of a particular piece of evidence is not recognized during the investigation, but becomes important when an unexpected defense theory is introduced. In most cases the evidence is not significant, and admitting a failure to document it can establish the witness' honesty — a characteristic of the witness that may actually enhance the police officer's credibility. On cross-examination, the defense attorney may point out measurements that were not made, observations that were not recorded, or details of the scene that were not included in the written police report, and then ask the question, "So your report is incomplete, isn't it?" The proper response (if it is truthful) should be: "For the purposes for which I was preparing the report, I consider it to be complete."

SAMPLE DIRECT TESTIMONY:

Q. Officer, was there any evidence at the scene that you did not document at the time, but that subsequently has been mentioned as possibly being significant?

A. Well, the left front tire from the defendant's vehicle was off the car when we processed the scene, but I didn't make a measurement to document where the tire was found.

Q. And why didn't you make such measurements at the time?

A. I didn't feel that the location of the tire was important to my reconstruction of the speed of the defendant's vehicle.

Q. Do you feel today as though the location of the left front tire would have any impact on your calculations?

A. No, I do not, it's just a piece of evidence, but it would not affect my calculations in any way.

§ 3-7(b). Expert's Opinion Differs From Testimony of Civilian Witness.

While it will very often be the case that an expert's opinion will differ from the testimony of a civilian witness, it should be dealt with and explained to the jury rather than being misused by the defense attorney as an attack on the credibility of the reconstruction. In fact, a witness' ability to accurately describe what was observed is affected by his/her use of language. It is therefore not unusual for several witnesses to the same event to describe it differently in some aspect. The police witness can help the jury understand this so the appropriate weight can be given to the testimony of the civilian witnesses and the reconstruction calculations done by the police witness. If this is not discussed in the direct examination, it may be used very effectively to attack the reconstruction opinion(s) by playing on the common sense of the jurors with a well-constructed question string.

SAMPLE TESTIMONY:

Q. Officer, did you speak with the civilian witnesses as part of your investigation and reconstruction of this crash?

A. Yes, I did.

Q. And after completing your calculations, did you again review the statements the witnesses gave to the police?

A. Yes.

Q. Are any of the observations that the witnesses made in their written statements not in agreement with your reconstruction of the crash?

A. Yes, but there is disagreement among the various witnesses.

Q. Does the fact that the witnesses disagree with your calculations cause you to want to change any of your opinions in this case?

A. No, my calculations are based on physical evidence and measurements at the scene, and I believe they have a high degree of certainty.

§ 3-7(c). Calculations Could Not Be Corroborated.

The calculations could not be corroborated by additional calculations using other reconstruction methodologies. In cases where sufficient evidence is found at the scene, the reconstruction may be done by several independent methods, such as momentum, energy, time-distance, etc. When this is done, the results of various methods corroborate each other and give greater certainty to the ultimate opinions reached in the reconstruction. However, in many cases there is not enough evidence to use a second method to reconstruct the crash, but this should not be interpreted as a lack of certainty in the calculations. By explaining to the jury that the physical evidence was limited in some way, the witness shows honesty in testifying that, while additional calculations would have been desirable, the lack thereof does not affect his/her opinion(s).

SAMPLE TESTIMONY:

Q. Officer, were you able to do any other calculations to determine the speed of the defendant's vehicle?

A. No, there wasn't any evidence to do additional calculations.

Q. Do you usually use more than one method to reconstruct a crash?

A. Sometimes, but usually the limited amount of available evidence doesn't allow that.

Q. Does limited evidence affect your confidence in the calculations that you were able to do?

A. No.

Q. Would you explain that to the jury?

A. Well, the energy method that I used in this case is widely accepted by reconstructionists, and not being able to do additional calculations doesn't diminish the accuracy or validity of the calculations that I was able to do.

Trial Tip

In such an instance, the witness should state confidently that although a corroborating calculation was not possible, the opinion is offered with certainty, without any sense of apology or misgiving.

---

§ 3-7(d). Reconstructionist Not Present at Scene.

The reconstructionist was not present at the scene, and therefore had to rely on measurements made by other investigators.

This might be attacked by the defense and portrayed as a "garbage in, garbage out" situation, but the reality is that the scene was processed using standard techniques, and that the measurements were exactly the same as the reconstructionist would have made if he/she had been at the scene. The prosecutor should emphasize the fact that the witness would not expect to have any additional or different information if he/she had personally processed the scene.

§ 3-7(e). Witness a Crash Reconstructionist Not Expert in Other Areas.

The witness (testifying as a crash reconstructionist) is not an expert in other areas, such as biomechanics, mechanical failure, tire failure analysis, brake operation and efficiency, human factors, etc. The witness, who is staying within the boundaries of his/her own expertise, may be attacked during cross-examination as not having expertise in areas related to crash reconstruction. By explaining the limits of his/her own expertise, the witness can show honesty and at the same time explain what other areas of expertise are, and that they are not necessary to reach the opinion(s) he/she offered in the direct testimony.

SAMPLE TESTIMONY:

Q. Officer, can you tell the jury the basis for your conclusions?

A. They are based on the use of widely accepted equations and methods of crash reconstruction.

Q. You aren't putting yourself forward to be an expert in brake operation, are you?

A. No.

Q. Can you tell the jury what human factors is?

A. In connection with motor vehicle crashes, it is the study of how people perceive, process information, make decisions, and react in certain situations.

Q. Do you consider yourself an expert in human factors?

A. Well no, but I am familiar with certain aspects of human factors, such as perception-reaction time, visibility sight distance, etc.

Q. Officer, do you believe that you need any of those other specific areas of expertise to offer the opinion(s) you have given here today?

A. No.

Q. Would you please explain why to the jury?

A. Well, the reconstruction that I did started with the physical evidence gathered at the scene, and....

§ 3-7(f). No Statement From Defendant.

The reconstructionist did not talk to or take a statement from the defendant or a witness friendly to the defendant prior to reaching conclusions about the speed of the defendant's vehicle, the path of travel, etc.

This is not uncommon, since the defendant is represented by counsel and usually would not continue to discuss the case with police. The intuitively obvious inference that the reconstructionist should have communicated with the defendant to get input from someone who was involved in the crash needs to be explained by the witness.

§ 3-7(g). Unprepared Witness.

The witness has not read a transcript or has not seen a particular exhibit prior to his/her taking the witness stand.

This occurs in the normal flow of information, especially when a civil action may be linked to the criminal case. The prosecutor should try to make any depositions available to the witness before trial, as there may be information that would be helpful to the reconstructionist. Sometimes a witness comes forward and speaks directly to the prosecutor or to an officer other than the witness. If this happens, it should be explained to the jury so that the defense does not use it as a surprise during cross, or as a way of inferring incompleteness on the part of the witness. The nature of this inoculation is to have the witness confirm that the additional information, statements, photographs, etc. are consistent with the witness' analysis and opinion(s) reached prior to trial, or at least are not reasons to change any of the opinions being offered.

SAMPLE TESTIMONY:

Q. Officer, I show you some photographs marked Exhibits 14 through 23. Have you seen those photographs prior to your testimony here today?

A. No I have not.

Q. Can you describe what you see in the photographs?

A. Yes, they are pictures of the damage to the defendant's vehicle and to the cement wall at the crash scene.

Q. Are the photographs similar to those taken by police during the investigation of this crash?

A. Yes, they appear to be very similar.

Q. Is there anything in these photographic exhibits that is different from the information you gathered during your investigation?

A. No.

Q. Does anything in these photographs cause you to make any change in any of your testimony or opinions in this case?

A. No.

§ 3-7(h). No Tests Performed on Vehicles Involved in Crash.

If no tests were performed on the vehicles involved in the crash, an inference may be made during cross-examination that a failure to do tests or operate the vehicles involved in the crash infers limited accuracy of the testimony. The officer should be prepared to comment on the foundation for his/her testimony and to state that the inability to operate the damaged vehicles would not change his/her conclusions.

The police witness must establish credibility and maintain it during both direct and cross-examination. By understanding how the jury perceives witnesses, the officer can offer testimony in a manner and style that promotes credibility. The route to being an effective witness can be shortened by knowing what traits the jury associates with credibility, and by consciously addressing those considerations.

References

(1) NHTSA, DOT HS 178, DWI Detection and Standardized Field Sobriety Testing (June 1992).
(2) NHTSA, DOT 805-864, V. Tharp, M. Burns & H. Moskowitz, Development of Field Test of Psychophysical Testing for DWI Arrest (March 1981).
(3) NHTSA, DOT HS 806-512, Impairment Sobriety Testing (1984).
(4) NHTSA DOT HS 806-475, T. Anderson, R. Schweitz & R. Snyder, Field Evaluation of a Behavioral Test Battery for DWI (September 1983).
(5) NHTSA DOT HS 802-424, M. Burns & H. Moskowitz, Psychophysical Tests for DWI Arrest (June 1977).
(6) J. Stapleton, et al., Effects of Alcohol and Other Psychotropic Drugs on Eye Movements: Relevance to Traffic Safety, 47 J Stud. On Alcohol 426, 427 (1986).
(7) M. Burns, The Controversy and the Issues: Horizontal Gaze Nystagmus, The DRE, Vol. 4, Issue 5 at 7 (October/November 1992).

Chapter 4

CROSS-EXAMINATION

§ 4-1. Cross-Examination — What the Police Witness Needs to Know.
§ 4-2. Cross-Examinations Dictate Case Outcomes.
§ 4-3. Two Types of Cross-Examination.
    § 4-3(a). General Areas of Attack on Police Witnesses.
    § 4-3(b). Attacking the Police Witness' Perception and/or Memory of an Event.
    § 4-3(c). Prior Inconsistent Statements.
    § 4-3(d). Bias, Prejudice, and Motivation.
    § 4-3(e). Incompetence.
§ 4-4. Specific Attack Strategies for Traffic Officers.
§ 4-5. Attack Strategies Commonly Used Against Drug Recognition Experts.
§ 4-6. Common Attacks on Police Accident Reconstructionists.
§ 4-7. Control.
    § 4-7(a). The Use of Leading Questions.
    § 4-7(b). The Use of Headlines.
    § 4-7(c). Interrupting the Witness.
    § 4-7(d). Intimidation.
    § 4-7(e). Using the Judge.
    § 4-7(f). Use of a Document.
§ 4-8. Witness Strategies to Counter the Cross-Examination.
    § 4-8(a). Witness Control of Time.
    § 4-8(b). Defense Attorney Incompetence.
        § 4-8(b)(1). When Defense Attorney Fails to Listen.
        § 4-8(b)(2). When Defense Attorney Lacks Questioning Capacity.
    § 4-8(c). Applying Visualization in Cross-Examination.
§ 4-9. In-Depth Analysis of Strategies Used in Reconstruction.
    § 4-9(a). Witness Knowledge/Competency.
    § 4-9(b). Incomplete or Faulty Investigation.
    § 4-9(c). Errors in Investigation or Reconstruction.
    § 4-9(d). Attacks on the Certainty of Opinion(s).

§ 4-1. Cross-Examination — What the Police Witness Needs to Know.

In order to be a witness capable of surviving cross-examination, the police witness needs to understand:

- the risks inherent in being cross-examined in a criminal case;
- the types of tactics defense counsel commonly use;
- the skills the defense attorney relies on to execute those tactics; and
- the methods available to the police witness to counter the tactics.

§ 4-2. Cross-Examinations Dictate Case Outcomes.

Some police officers have greater anxiety about being cross-examined in court by a defense attorney than any other aspect of their work. There are some very legitimate reasons for this anxiety:

- cross-examinations of key witnesses in criminal cases are nearly always "outcome determinative" — successful cross-examinations win cases;
- the defense attorney's successful cross-examination of just one key prosecution witness may be sufficient to generate a reasonable doubt and a not guilty verdict in the case;
- defense attorneys tend to be more openly aggressive and hostile towards a police witness than to other types of witnesses;
- people in our culture (including jurors) pay greater attention, remember longer and give greater weight to negative information than positive;
- a police officer with a clear perception of the objective reality of a case, one that shows the defendant's criminal culpability, represents a major obstacle to any potential success of any defense theory;
- witnesses, police officers specifically, often feel that cross-examination is a personal attack on their character; and
- most witnesses feel helpless during cross-examination, as if they have no power to counter the cross-examination attack without becoming argumentative and looking stupid.

Trial Tip

In an aggressive cross-examination, confrontation between a defense attorney and a police witness, jurors will select a winner and loser when it is done. The winner will be the one whose visual image of their case the jurors carry with them into the jury room. If the police witness' picture of reality prevails after the defense attack, more often than not there will be a conviction.

At the end of the cross-examination, the jurors can usually identify a winner and a loser.

§ 4-3. Two Types of Cross-Examination.

There are essentially two reasons why defense attorneys cross-examine any witness. One reason is to use the witness to support some aspect of the defense theory. This is called an **affirmative** cross-examination. The second reason a defense attorney cross-examines a witness is to attempt to weaken the government's case. This is called a **destructive** cross-examination. When the cross-examiner is able to weaken the credibility of the police witness, it is called impeachment. The focus of this chapter is on destructive cross-examinations.

> **Trial Tip**
>
> *The Order of Cross-Exam. When a competent defense attorney has both a line of affirmative cross-examination questions and a line of destructive cross-examination questions available, he/she will almost always conduct the affirmative cross-examination first.*

§ 4-3(a). General Areas of Attack on Police Witnesses.

To some degree, all police witnesses are subject to attack on their credibility. No one is perfectly objective, or a perfect observer, recorder, or reporter of an event. No one does everything that is theoretically possible to be done to investigate an event. Police behavior may be inconsistent with logic or circumstance or the law or be made to appear inconsistent in those ways. Police may even exhibit or express a bias or prejudice in relation to different sides of a dispute. Because police officers are human, as witnesses they are vulnerable to destructive cross-examination attacks. In the following sections, various attack approaches are identified and explained.

> **Trial Tip**
>
> *Inoculation and Redirect Examination. Any cross-examination attack on a police officer can be anticipated and countered in advance during the direct examination. Any attack not handled on direct may be countered on redirect examination.*

§ 4-3(b). Attacking the Police Witness' Perception and/or Memory of an Event.

There might have been insufficient time, lighting, or visibility to see the event (that resulted in a criminal charge) accurately; the officer could have had little sleep; the officer could have been juggling two or three serious, even life-threatening circumstances at the time; or, the officer was too inexperienced or insufficiently trained to make an accurate assessment of what was being observed. Maybe weeks, months, or years have passed since the event, or the officer may have had many cases since the events occurred.

§ 4-3(c). Prior Inconsistent Statements.

The officer appears to have given different testimony about the case in a prior court proceeding, deposition, or administrative hearing. The officer's report, by either omission or commission, appears to contradict his or her court testimony.

§ 4-3(d). Bias, Prejudice, and Motivation.

The officer chose to believe other witnesses rather than the defendant without a rational basis for doing so; the officer wants a conviction more than justice; the officer isn't fair because of the defendant's race, background, relations, or other credibility-costly reason.

§ 4-3(e). Incompetence.

The officer uses poor investigation technique, makes an incomplete or poor report, or is inconsistent with other officers, etc. Audio or video equipment was available to record some of the officer's observations, especially of the defendant's behavior, but was not used.

§ 4-4. Specific Attack Strategies for Traffic Officers.

In addition to the general attacks outlined in the above section, some of the areas of cross-examination commonly used with patrol officers include:

(1) The officer's account differs from the civilian eyewitnesses (often defendant's friends);

(2) The officer's investigation is incomplete in some detail (which the defense attorney will later claim would have exposed the reality of the case to the jury had the officer conducted that missing part of the investigation);

(3) The officer was not present (when the "fender bender" occurred and is relying upon other people's word);

(4) The officer did not photograph or diagram the vehicles involved in the event;

(5) The officer has limited training, experience or education and the quality of the officer's work is suspect;

(6) The witness who did not take photographs is confronted with photographs and/or diagrams made by the defendant or someone sympathetic to the defense;

(7) An officer of limited experience and training did not confer with any more experienced or better trained senior officer about the case;.

(8) The officer did not speak with the defendant or the defendant's colleagues or companions prior to writing the charge;

(9) The witness is unfamiliar with his/her prior testimony or police report in the case; or

(10) The officer was completely unaware that a particular witness in the case existed.

§ 4-5. Attack Strategies Commonly Used Against Drug Recognition Experts.

(a) DRE witnesses have never been permitted to testify in the trial courts in the state of X;

(b) The DRE program is not taught in the police academies of the state;

(c) The DRE is not a medical doctor; has not attended any medical schools; is not a physician's assistant, registered nurse, or had any comparable training; is not a paramedic or even an EMT;

(d) The DRE was not taught his/her expertise by certified medical personnel;

(e) The DRE cannot define the technical medical terms which arguably relate to the diagnostic aspects of the drug influence examination;

(f) The DRE may not be able to competently give psycho-physiological cause-effect explanations for his/her observations;

(g) If the DRE believed the defendant was under the influence of a drug, the DRE had a moral responsibility to secure an attorney and obtain medical care for the defendant;

(h) If the defendant was under the influence of a drug, how could this defendant give a knowing and intelligent consent to being touched by the DRE in a manner similar to the way a trained doctor or nurse touches a patient; and

(i) Where the DRE witness and the defendant were of the opposite sex and where the DRE witness was not careful to have a third person present during all the stages of the drug recognition protocol, implications of impropriety are available to the defense attorney.

§ 4-6. Common Attacks on Police Accident Reconstructionists.

Some of the most highly trained police officers in a department are the accident reconstructionists. They are commonly involved in every vehicular crash in a jurisdiction where death or serious injury has resulted. Rather than being immune to defense cross-examination strategies, these witnesses offer larger targets for attack. In addition to all of the strategies identified in the prior sections, additional attacks are set forth below:

(1) The officer's credentials are weak in any formal education in accident reconstruction;
(2) The officer lacks on-the-job training or experience;
(3) The officer has no experience in cases with facts like the case being tried;
(4) The credentials of the officer are inferior to the credentials of the defense expert (education, training, experience, board certification, etc.);
(5) The officer did not have access to important information;
(6) The officer knew of tests and measurements that could have been done but were not;
(7) The officer lacks knowledge of how the measurements he or she is relying on were obtained;
(8) There were other ways to compute defendant's speed that might have yielded a lower number;
(9) The officer accepted a patrol officer's characterization that the marks measured were yaw marks rather than skid marks, or vice versa, (he/she has never inspected the marks), and the choice of which type of mark has a significant impact on the result;
(10) The witness has made certain "assumptions" in making the calculations because the actual facts were not available;
(11) The officer has given training programs to police and prosecutor audiences and has never done similar presentations for defense attorneys;
(12) The methodologies the officer utilized in the case are disapproved of by recognized authorities in the expert's field;
(13) The officer either made no report or a very poorly prepared report; and
(14) The expert cannot testify that the victim's driving or some other intervening event was not a causal factor in a crash.

§ 4-7. Control.

For any defense attack strategy on a witness to succeed and to be understood and appreciated by the jury, the defense attorney must control the witness — force the witness to answer the questions the way the defense attorney wants the questions answered. Without control, the defense attorney would be trying to hit a moving target. Throughout every cross-examination is a hidden and unspoken battle between the witness and the defense attorney over who controls the witness' testimony.

Defense attorneys fall into patterns on how they attempt to control witnesses on cross-examination, and the subject of how a particular defense attorney tries to achieve control should be discussed by the police witness and prosecutor before trial. The greater the witness' understanding of the defense attorney's control tactics, the less likely the witness will display frustration, resentment, or other credibility-costly attitudes in front of the jury during cross-examination. A list of control techniques with explanations of each is set forth in the following sections.

Trial Tip

The Self-Destructive Witness. Police witnesses who tend to react strongly to any form of control in social situations and whose testimony has not been well-prepared, often display to the jury their open hostility and aggressiveness towards the defense attorney. Unjustified anger destroys credibility and is rarely excused by jurors.

Basic Control Techniques:

§ 4-7(a). The Use of Leading Questions.

Short, simple, well-framed, leading questions direct the witness to the desired answer, almost always a "yes" or "no."

Example: "You didn't see the crash happen, did you?"
"You didn't know my client before that night?"
"You didn't smell alcohol, did you?

§ 4-7(b). The Use of Headlines.

Headlines tell the witness where the cross-examiner is going, using a statement to set up a question. There is nothing a witness can do about the attorney who uses "statement" headlines, and there is usually nothing the witness needs to do. Headlines do not control as much as they tend to fortify the question that follows the headline.

Example: "Let's talk about the extent of your police training."
"Let's look at the reason you stopped my client."

§ 4-7(c). Interrupting the Witness.

The defense attorney will try to stop the witness as soon as the desired portion of an answer is given. The attorney will attempt this in several ways: (1) by inserting a "thank you" or "excuse me"; (2) by starting a new question at the strategic point in the witness' answer; or (3) by using a STOP sign gesture (holding an arm out with the palm open and pointing up) towards the witness. These techniques are strengthened by the defense attorney formally "objecting" to the judge that the witness is being unresponsive or is volunteering answers.

§ 4-7(d). Intimidation.

Some defense attorneys believe they can intimidate witnesses into being more easily controlled by invading the witness' space or by raising their voices.

§ 4-7(e). Using the Judge.

Some defense attorneys will ask the judge to instruct a witness to answer their questions with a "yes" or a "no." Where the question is very well-crafted and clear in meaning, some judges will give that instruction. Many defense attorneys avoid using this technique because most judges tend either to advise the witness to answer with a yes or no "if they can" or to "answer as best they can."

§ 4-7(f). Use of a Document.

Some defense attorneys will use the police report to control the witness, reading a phrase or sentence out of context and asking the police witness if he or she didn't write those words or make those statements. This is an improper method of questioning a witness that unfortunately is allowed in many courts. Whenever a defense attorney appears to be reading from a document and asks the witness to adopt the contents of the reading, the witness should request to see the document and should carefully review the document before answering any questions about it.

Trial Tip

Composure. More than at any other time in his or her professional life, the officer must maintain composure during cross-examination. The more argumentative or evasive an officer is while answering questions, the more that officer will be perceived as prejudiced and deceptive, undeserving of the jury's trust.

---

§ 4-8. Witness Strategies to Counter the Cross-Examination.

A witness is not helpless during cross-examination. They have control over certain important aspects of the question-answer process that cannot be taken away. They can also take advantage of a defense attorney's incompetencies.

Finally, if they can visualize their work in a case, they can employ a four-step method in answering the defense attorney's questions that is very powerful.

§ 4-8(a). Witness Control of Time.

All witnesses start with control of three things: (1) Time — the witness controls how quickly and at what pace they answer the defense attorney's questions; (2) Truth — by filtering all questions through their mind's eye picture of the investigation, and by ensuring that his or her vocabulary accurately fits the mental picture, the truth becomes very easy to protect from distortion; and (3) Temper or attitude, which the witness must always keep in check.

Regarding the timing/tempo of the question-answer process during a cross-examination, the law does not require a witness to answer a question at the same pace it was asked by the attorney. The faster the witness answers, the sooner the next question will be asked, and the more likely the witness will trip up. The witness can take as long as he/she needs to respond.

The value of the witness' control over time may become more apparent when one examines how a cross-examination is constructed. Most cross-examinations consist of a very few lines of inquiry, like pillars on a bridge — a bridge the defense attorney tries to build from the witness' version of events to the defense's version. Each question that the defense attorney asks builds upon the answer to the previous question, and without the answer that he/she wants from the witness, the question string cannot continue.

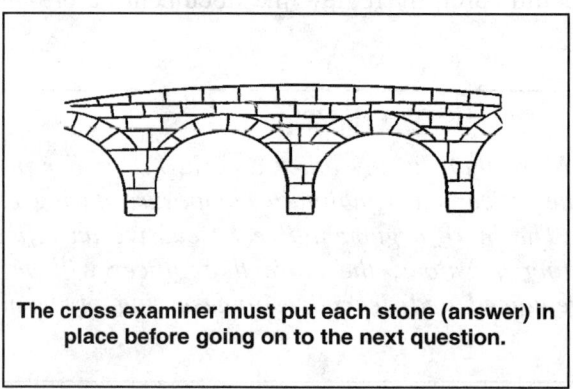

The cross examiner must put each stone (answer) in place before going on to the next question.

If the witness does not give the exact answer upon which the following question rests or does not answer in a timely manner, the examiner must make a decision on whether to be patient or whether to move on to another line of questioning. Attorneys want fast answers and they want their lines of questions to develop at a pace the jurors can follow. A witness is under no obligation to assist the defense attorney in this task.

Trial Tip

A witness is not confined to answering yes or no to the defense attorney's questions when they unfairly mislead or contain false information. Unless instructed otherwise by the judge, witnesses are free to qualify their answers: "Your question is partly right." "May I explain?" "That depends."

---

§ 4-8(b). Defense Attorney Incompetence.

In addition to control, there are two other important trial advocacy skills a defense attorney must possess. They are: (1) the ability to accurately listen and strategically react to courtroom testimony; and (2) the ability to frame simple and easy-to-understand questions. The police witness is under no obligation to help the defense attorney.

§ 4-8(b)(1). When Defense Attorney Fails to Listen.

Additional opportunities for a witness to control the cross-examination occur when the defense attorney is not carefully listening to the witness' testimony. The police witness who realizes that the defense attorney is not paying attention to the answers can respond to the cross-examination questions in a manner that further fortifies the factual information the officer recited on direct. The cross-examination becomes merely an extenuation of the direct examination.

§ 4-8(b)(2). When Defense Attorney Lacks Questioning Capacity.

Until the defense attorney demonstrates the ability to ask the police witness an understandable question, the witness has no obligation to give any type of answer. Framing clear, simple questions is very difficult to do. Inexperience, nervousness, incompetence, or mental lapses of the attorney leave a witness invulnerable to attack.

§ 4-8(c). Applying Visualization in Cross-Examination.

Using visualization, the officer can instantly rebel against any effort, subtle or otherwise, to distort his or her perception of reality. Leading questions have an inherent capacity for highlighting the slightest distortion of the witness' picture. When police witnesses use their minds' eye to visualize their activities in a case, a very powerful, four-step technique is available to them that allows the witness to counter most cross-examination attacks, thereby preserving the witness' image of the case for the jury:

With regard to each question in a cross-examination, the following instructions apply:

(1) Using the subject matter of the defense attorney's question, form a picture of that aspect of the case where the information needed to answer the question is supposed to be;
(2) Determine whether anything about the question requires you to add or eliminate or in any manner distort this picture you are holding in your mind's eye of the case;
(3) If the question tends to distort your picture, make an assessment of how important the distortion is before answering the question;
(4) If the distortion is important, express that distortion as your answer; if it is a minor distortion, mention it in passing as you answer the question; and if it is insignificant, simply answer the defense attorney's question.

§ 4-9. In-Depth Analysis of Strategies Used in Reconstruction.

The careful analysis of actual courtroom cross-examination strategies is highly instructive, particularly with regard to a highly qualified police witness. The police-reconstructionist witness is ideal for dramatically illustrating ways a defense attorney's questioning can have an adverse impact on the credibility of a police officer, regardless of his or her credentials, experience, thoroughness, professionalism, or objectivity in any given case. Even though most of the defense strategies and the commentary relative to the strategies may be very specific to the reconstructionist-witness situation, all demonstrate the conceptual framework of the defense attorney's cross-examination strategy.

§ 4-9(a). Witness Knowledge/Competency.

(1) Can you cite a treatise to back up your statement?

Comment. The examiner is trying to show that the officer is poorly trained by asking him/her to quote the author and title of a literary reference to support some part of his/her prior testimony. It would not be uncommon for an officer, or even an expert witness, to be unable to do so off the top of his/her head under the pressure of the cross-examination.

Q. Officer, you stated in your direct exam that the launch angle for a motorcycle rider is usually less than 20 degrees measured from the horizontal. Do you remember making that statement?

A. Yes.

Q. And you used that assumption to make some of your calculations, didn't you?

A. Yes.

Q. In fact your entire calculation of the speed of the defendant was dependent on making that assumption, wasn't it?

A. Yes.

Q. Officer, that angle isn't something that you yourself measured, is it?

A. No.

Q. And you haven't done any tests yourself to determine that angle, have you?

A. No.

Q. You've stated that the launch angle you used in your calculations came from research that someone else did. Is that true?

A. Yes.

Q. Can you tell the jury where it came from?

A. Not right now, I can't remember.

Q. Did you bring the research article to court with you today?

A. No.

Q. And you don't know the name of the author or the title of the article as you sit here today?

A. No.

Comment. The witness should not have been so willing to say that the entire calculation depended on the assumption he/she made, but might have answered, "The assumption was to some degree of certainty and is based on my own training and experience, so I stand by it."

When confronted with a demand to name the author and title of the article, the witness could have responded, "I have the article and would be glad to bring it to court with me tomorrow (if that were the case), but I can't remember the information here and now."

(2) Why do you add the squares of speeds in the "combined speeds" equation?

Comment. The examiner is asking for an explanation of an equation that most police reconstructionists commonly use in their work. But many do not really know the origin of the equation or have not been taught the derivation of the equation as part of their training. This is an attempt to make the witness seem incompetent because he/she cannot readily derive a basic equation. The jury may think that the witness should be able to do so, if asked, and this may be an attack that must be addressed on redirect examination.

Q. Officer, you said in your direct testimony that you used an equation called the "combined speeds equation." Is that correct?

A. Yes.

Q. And you said you had been trained to use that equation?

A. Yes. It was part of my basic reconstruction class.

Q. In that equation you indicated that you square the speed of each event before adding it to the other speeds?

A. Yes. That's correct.

Q. Why do you do that? I mean, why do you square a speed before you add it to another speed?

A. Because that's what the equation says to do.

Q. But do you know the reason that the equation has squares in it in the first place?

A. No.

Q. Would it be fair to say that you've been trained to use the equation, but you don't know the basis for the equation with respect to the laws of physics and that sort of thing?

A. Well, I can't derive the equation from scratch. But I think it has something to do with the conservation of energy.

Q. But you don't know exactly where the equation comes from?

A. No.

Comment. Asking a witness to derive an equation may be a way of challenging the witness in the eye of the judge, but most officers would not be expected as part of their training to be able to derive such an equation. The officer should know, however, that squaring the speed makes it proportional to the energy of the particular event, and that what must really be added together are the energies of the events of the crash. An appropriate answer might be, "I don't know, but may I explain?" This would give the officer a chance to indicate that the equation is widely accepted, and can be found in almost all reconstruction texts, but that he/she was not particularly trained to derive the equation. The prosecutor should note this type of attack and be ready to address it during redirect if the witness has been seriously damaged by the attack. In most cases, jurors will accept that the officer has been trained to use the equation correctly, and may not expect a derivation of the equation from basic physics principles.

(3) What is the 30 in the "speed from skid marks equation"?

Comment. Again, the examiner uses this type of question to portray the witness as incompetent to the jury. Officers are usually taught that the number 30 is a "constant" in the equation, but may never have seen exactly where it comes from. The prosecutor should assess the damage that this attack has done, and address it in redirect, if necessary.

Q. Officer, you used an equation called the "speed from skid marks equation" to determine the speed of my client's vehicle. Is that correct?

A. Yes, I did.

Q. Can you write that equation on the board for the jurors?

A. Yes. (*Goes to board and writes equation.*)

Q. In the equation that you wrote there is a number 30 and some letters. Can you tell the jury why the number 30 appears in the equation?

A. It is a constant.

Q. What does that mean?

A. The number 30 is in the equation all the time, regardless of what vehicle is being analyzed.

Q. I guess I don't understand, but why is the number 30 in the equation? Why isn't it 26 or 35 or something else?

A. I don't know. It's just a constant. It is because of the acceleration of gravity.

Q. I don't remember much about my physics, but I thought that gravity was 32.2. You're not saying that the 30 is gravity, are you?

A. Well, it's that and some other things.

Q. What other things?

A. I don't really know.

Q. So you use this equation, but you don't know where it comes from?

A. I can't derive it right now.

Comment. This is a similar attack to the one discussed above. If the prosecutor knows that this attorney uses this tactic, he/she should prepare the officer for it ahead of time. It may be unfair to expect a witness to derive this on the stand, but the jury may expect a witness giving an expert opinion to be able to do so. Actually the 30 comes from the acceleration of gravity; a witness may be able to review the derivation and offer an answer in redirect testimony, but still explain that he/she was not trained to derive the equation or the value of the constant in the equation.

(4) Can the witness differentiate between coefficient of friction and drag factor?

Comment. This is a subtle distinction in some cases, but most officers should know the difference — coefficient of friction refers to the ratio of friction force to weight pressing two flat, horizontal surfaces together, while drag factor includes any effects of grade, super elevation, braking efficiency, etc.

Q. Officer, you mentioned the term "drag factor" in your direct testimony and indicated that it was an important part of your calculations of the speed of my client's vehicle. Is that correct?

A. Yes.

Q. And you said that you measured the drag factor yourself, in this case?

A. Yes, I did.

Q. Are you familiar with the term coefficient of friction?

A. Yes.

Q. Can you tell the jury how the coefficient of friction differs from the drag factor?

A. Well, they're essentially the same.

Q. Doesn't the drag factor include more information than the coefficient of friction?

A. No, they're the same thing in most cases.

Q. Then why are there two different names for the same thing?

A. One is a physics definition, and the other is the way reconstruction people talk about it.

Q. So your testimony is that the two terms mean exactly the same thing?

A. In most cases that's true.

Comment. The distinction between these two terms is very technical. The witness should explain what he/she knows about the distinction, and not go out on a limb trying to satisfy the examiner. The answer given in this example is adequate if the officer does not specifically know the difference between the two terms. This is information that a witness should be able to explain to the jury, though. The correct answer to the last question might be, "What I measured on the road surface included the grade and super elevation of the road, and therefore it was the drag factor."

(5) The witness has no formal training in physics. (Note: This question string may be intended to impress the judge with a lack of formal training, and lead to a motion to set aside the opinion(s) of the police witness. It might also be used to compare the defense expert witness to the police witness in the hope that the jury will give greater weight to a defense witness with higher credentials. The prosecutor must put this in its proper perspective during inoculation in the direct examination.)

Q. Officer, you have used a number of equations to reach your opinion about the speed of my client's car on the evening of the accident. And you have said that you received training to use those equations. Is that correct?

A. Yes, I had eighty hours of reconstruction and advanced reconstruction training.

Q. Can you tell the jury your education in the field of physics?

A. I haven't taken any physics courses.

Q. You'd agree with me that these equations come from basic physics, don't they?

A. Yes.

Q. And without any training in physics, you just have to accept the equations as being valid?

A. That's correct.

Q. So if there is any special consideration in using these equations, or any limitation on their use, you aren't aware of that, are you?

A. I was taught to use the equations in certain instances, and that's what I do.

Q. But you aren't aware of any limitations on the equations that are imposed as a result of the laws of physics from which the equations are derived?

A. No, I'm not aware of any limitations.

Q. So, in fact, there might be occasions where the equations could be misused if you weren't aware of such limitations. Isn't that correct?

A. I guess so.

Comment. The witness should stick with his/her assertion that he/she was trained to use the equations only when sufficient information is available. The witness does not have to acknowledge any alleged occasions where the equations could be misused. A better answer to the last question might be, "There might be occasions where the equations couldn't be used because of a lack of information, but I had everything I needed to do the calculations in this case."

§ 4-9(b). Incomplete or Faulty Investigation.

(1) The reconstructionist did not visit the scene.

Comment. This should not occur under most circumstances, but it may happen. The witness has no first-hand knowledge of the topography of the scene, visibility afforded to the operators, and/or other information. He/she does not have the best mental picture of the reconstructed crash, but is being asked, nonetheless, to offer testimony regarding the reconstruction calculations.

Q. Officer, you offered an opinion in your earlier testimony about the speed of my client's car on the night of the accident?

A. That's correct.

Q. And your opinion was reached using information about the scene, specifically the road surface, the grade of the road, and other information of that sort. Is that correct?

A. Yes.

Q. In most other cases that you have reconstructed in the past, it was important for you to visit the scene before reaching your conclusions. Isn't that true?

A. To some extent.

Q. But in this case you arrived at an opinion without even seeing the scene or walking along the roadway to get a feel for it?

A. That's right.

Q. You'd agree with me, wouldn't you, that it would have been better if you had visited the scene as part of your investigation before reaching your conclusion(s)?

A. Yes.

Comment. The examiner will characterize the witness' work as shoddy or incomplete in the closing argument, as he/she should in this case. But the witness (who felt he/she could reach an opinion to some degree of certainty without visiting the scene) could have explained that to the jury by answering the final question, "Yes, but may I explain?"

(2) The specific input of the driver may have affected the acceleration tests that the witness conducted. (Note: Since the acceleration tests yielded information that was the foundation for various calculations and opinions, the examiner tries to discredit the accuracy of the tests and to show the jury that the specific results using this driver should not be directly applied to the client in this case.)

> Q. Officer, you said in your prior testimony that you did some acceleration tests to get data for your calculations?
>
> A. That's correct.
>
> Q. And you said that you used a vehicle that closely matched the vehicle my client was operating on the evening of the accident. Is that correct?
>
> A. Yes.
>
> Q. And you did that so that the tests would be as close as possible to the conditions of the accident that we have been considering. Isn't that true?
>
> A. Yes.
>
> Q. Who was the driver in the tests that you did?
>
> A. I was assisted by Officer Jones.
>
> Q. And you didn't give him any special instructions about how to operate the car during the tests, did you?
>
> A. No.
>
> Q. And you didn't speak with my client before you did the tests to get any information about how he was driving, did you?
>
> A. No.
>
> Q. So your tests depended very much on whatever Officer Jones did, didn't they?
>
> A. His driving behavior and the capabilities of the car. That's correct.
>
> Q. As you sit here today you can't be certain that Officer Jones drove exactly the same way as my client did that night, can you?

A. I feel confident that he did the best he could to drive the way your client did.

Comment. This attack is based on the common sense that the examiner feels the jury will have, but if the tests were done with a variety of driving behaviors, the witness would have had a range of data to use in subsequent calculations. The opinion resulting from the tests would have then included a range of possible outcomes, and the officer would have been less vulnerable to attack during cross-examination.

(3) The witness did not review the timing pattern of the traffic light controlling the intersection where the crash occurred. (Note: This attack is meant to show that the witness is not capable of understanding the timing pattern or that the investigation is incomplete. The focus of the cross may depend on how the witness answers the questions.)

Q. Officer, this accident took place at an intersection. Is that correct?

A. That's correct.

Q. And the intersection was controlled by a standard traffic signal. Is that correct?

A. Yes.

Q. You said that you personally observed that the traffic signal was working when you were at the scene?

A. That's correct.

Q. And you included that information in your written report, didn't you?

A. Yes.

Q. You included that information because you thought it was pertinent to how the accident occurred, didn't you?

A. Yes.

Q. Now, are you familiar with what is called a timing pattern for traffic signals?

A. Yes.

Q. Can you tell the jury what a timing pattern chart is?

A. It is a chart that shows....

Q. Did you obtain as part of your investigation the timing chart for the traffic signal at this intersection?

A. No.

Q. So you never checked to see if the timing sequence of the signal was correct. You just know that the signal was changing from one color to another. Isn't that correct?

A. Yes.

Q. Officer, if the lights had changed at the wrong time or in the wrong sequence, couldn't that have caused my client to enter the intersection without expecting the other vehicle to also have a green light?

A. I guess so.

Comment. The examiner has tried to show that the investigation was incomplete, and has introduced the hypothetical that the lights were both green at the same time. The witness must continually run the questions through his/her picture of the crash; in this case there was no indication that the timing sequence was wrong or that both operators had green lights, so the better answer to the final question might have been, "I don't understand the question. Are you saying that the signal was operating wrong and that the signal was green in both directions at the same time?" The examiner will not, without foundation, suggest that such was the case, and the witness will avoid confirming the hypothetical.

(4) The measuring equipment used in the investigation was not calibrated before and after it was used. (Note: The examiner is suggesting that the measurements are incorrect, and that calculations using those measurements are therefore wrong. In many cases this is the only attack on speed estimates and other reconstruction opinions, because the defense expert would reach the same conclusion as the state's witness if both used the same numbers.)

Q. Officer, you testified earlier that you made many measurements with what is called a rolling wheel?

A. That's correct.

Q. Isn't it possible to check the accuracy of your rolling wheel by comparing it to a tape measure laid out on the ground?

A. Yes.

Q. And you're aware of that method of checking the rolling wheel, aren't you?

A. Yes.

Q. Did you do that in this case?

A. No, I didn't.

Q. Wouldn't that have been a way for you to know for sure that the rolling wheel was working correctly that day?

A. Yes.

Q. But you didn't do that in this case, did you?

A. No.

Q. So as you sit here today you can't say with any certainty that the measurements are correct, can you?

A. I've used the wheel since then and I have not had any problem with it.

Q. But you didn't check it that day, did you?

A. No.

Comment. The examiner has challenged the foundation for the witness' calculations, and has suggested that the measuring wheel may have malfunctioned that day. The witness could avoid this hypothetical by calibrating the instrument every time he/she uses it. If this attack seems to be particularly troublesome, the prosecutor may clarify the witness' testimony during redirect.

(5) The officer did not check to see if there was any recall (or did not know that there was a recall) on the defendant's vehicle, or if any mechanical defect or condition may been a possible cause of the crash. (Note: This is one of the first things that some investigators check in a MV collision, especially if the operator had mentioned some apparent problem with his/her vehicle prior to the crash. The mechanical failure defense often surfaces much later in the life of the case, and is only as successful as the incompleteness of the investigation, the failure to secure the vehicle as evidence, etc.)

Q. Officer, you filed a written report of this accident on June 12, 19__. Isn't that true?

A. Yes.

Q. And in your report you didn't mention any investigation or consideration that my client's vehicle may have malfunctioned and caused this accident, did you?

A. No.

Q. You're aware, aren't you, that from time to time a certain model or make of car is recalled because there is a mechanical problem with the car?

A. Yes, I'm aware of that.

Q. You'd agree that a complete investigation would have included a check to see if my client's vehicle had any such mechanical problem?

A. That depends.

Q. But you didn't consider that possibility in this case, did you?

A. I didn't have any reason to expect a mechanical problem with your client's car.

Q. So in that respect your investigation of this accident is incomplete, isn't it?

A. I guess so.

Comment. The officer should not leave the jury with the conclusion that the investigation is incomplete. He/she could have answered in a manner that did not leave that impression, such as "I didn't expect a mechanical problem then, and I still don't have any reason to believe there was such a problem."

(6) The officer did not include in his report any attempt to look for road defects that might have caused the collision. (Note: Although the officer did walk the scene to inspect the road for defects — potholes, edge drop-off, etc. — he did not include any mention of that investigation in his written report. The defense attorney attacks the lack of any mention of such investigation as an indication that the investigation was incomplete, suggesting that there is a possibility such a defect did exist and could have caused the crash.)

Q. Officer, how long were you at the scene?

A. About two hours.

Q. And you were the chief investigator, in charge of processing the scene for evidence?

A. Yes.

Q. Did you prepare a written report in this case?

A. Yes.

Q. Is this a copy of your complete written report?

A. Yes.

Q. You'd agree with me, wouldn't you, that there is no mention in your written report of any attempt to look for any road defect that might have been a factor in this accident?

A. There isn't any mention of it in my written report, but I did look for defects.

Q. Then the answer to my question is that there is no mention of any attempt to look for defects in your written report?

A. Yes.

Q. And isn't it your responsibility to include in your report any part of your investigation that is important?

A. That depends on what you mean by "important."

Q. So you didn't think that a possible road defect that might have been a cause of this accident was important enough to put into your report?

A. There wasn't any road defect, but I didn't bother writing that in my report.

Comment. This answer tells the jury that the issue of a possible road defect is without basis, since the officer did inspect the road during his investigation, but did not report the lack of such an observation in his written report.

(7) The reconstructionist did not determine the critical speed for a curve just prior to location of the crash. (Note: This would have placed an upper limit on the speed of the defendant's vehicle as it negotiated that curve. The defense attorney hopes to show that the failure to do this calculation shows that the officer is biased, since that calculation should have been consistent with the reconstructionist's opinion regarding the speed of the defendant's vehicle.)

Q. Can you describe the nature of the road just prior to the point where this accident occurred?

A. There is a curve about 500 feet before the point where your client's car left the road and went into the trees.

Q. Are you familiar with a calculation called "critical speed for a curve"?

A. Yes.

Q. Would you explain what that calculation is to the jury?

A. It is a calculation by which you can determine....

Q. Have you been trained to do that calculation, and have you done it in other cases?

A. Yes.

Q. Did you do that calculation for the curve just before the location of the accident in this case?

A. No.

Q. Wouldn't that calculation have confirmed your estimate of the speed of my client's vehicle if you had done it?

A. Well, it would have given a speed consistent with my estimate of speed.

Q. But you didn't do that calculation that would have corroborated your estimate of the speed of my client's vehicle?

A. No, I didn't.

Comment. The defense attorney will argue that the failure to do the critical speed calculation was intentional because it would have cast doubt on the officer's speed estimate. The officer should have alerted the prosecutor to revisit this issue in redirect examination by answering, "No, but may I explain?"

(8) The defense attorney attacks the weight of the vehicle that was used in the calculations. (Note: The exact weight of a vehicle is not usually a significant factor in calculations, and changing the weight by fifty to 100 pounds in a sensitivity analysis usually does not produce a significant change in the calculations.)

Q. Officer, you said that you used a weight of 2,560 lbs. for my client's vehicle when you did your calculations. Is that correct?

A. Yes.

Q. Can you tell the jury the weight of the gasoline that was in the gas tank? The weight of the occupants of the vehicle? The weight of any cargo that was in the trunk of my client's car?

A. Not exactly.

Q. So how did you determine the weight of my client's vehicle to be 2,560 lbs. for your calculations?

A. I estimated it from the vehicle specifications.

Q. If I were to tell you that the correct weight of the vehicle might have been as much as 3,120 lbs., would that make a difference to you?

A. I could use that number and do my calculations again, if you'd like.

Q. But you already gave your opinion, and when you did you said it was to "some degree of scientific certainty," didn't you?

A. Yes, I did.

Q. And now you're saying that if you were wrong by more than 20% about the weight of my client's vehicle you would be willing to redo the calculations. You'd agree with me, wouldn't you, that if you were wrong about the numbers you used in your calculations, then the results of those calculations were wrong, too?

A. Yes, but I'm not sure how different the calculations would be.

Comment. The defense attorney has just planted the idea in the jurors' minds that the speed estimate in earlier testimony was probably wrong. The officer very subtly accepted the fact that the correct weight of the defendant's vehicle could have been 3,120 lbs. — he/she should have known going into trial that such a difference was not possible, and answered in a more conversational style when that question was originally asked in the examination, "Are you telling me that the weight of your client's vehicle was 3,120 lbs.?" Once the 3,120 lbs. has been allowed to enter the "picture," it may influence the jurors' assessment of the credibility of the witness, or one of them may overestimate its importance in the calculation. The officer should have done a sensitivity analysis with weight as a variable to eliminate this type of attack.

(9) The defense attorney challenges the police photographs because the officer didn't document the specifics about the camera, lens, film, printing process, etc. (Note: The best way to head off this attack is to document the information relating to the photographs as a standard part of the investigation.)

Q. Let's talk about the photographs that you took. You'd agree with me that in order for the photographs to be of any help, they have to be a fair and accurate representation of what you would see with your eye?

A. Yes.

Q. And in that regard it would be important to be sure that the film accurately reproduced the colors and sharpness of the real images?

A. Yes.

Q. What kind of film and what speed film did you use to take these photographs?

A. I'm not sure, but I usually use Kodak 200 speed film.

Q. And what type lens did you have on your camera when you took these pictures?

A. I think it was a 50 mm focal length lens.

(Note: A series of exacting questions about the exposure time, developing process, printing process, type of paper used, etc., follows.)

Q. So, as you sit here today, Officer, you'd have to agree that you really don't know very much about the equipment and process that was used to make these photographs?

A. Well, I've been taking pictures this way for years now.

Q. But without knowing much about the equipment and process used to make these photographs, you can't say with any certainty that they accurately represent what you saw with your eyes that day at the scene?

A. I'd have to disagree with you, sir. My testimony is that they do represent accurately what I saw with my eyes that day.

Comment. Additional attacks that suggest the investigation was incomplete or faulty, or that the conclusions were based on faulty calculations, might include:

(10) The officer was not able to inspect the vehicles involved in the crash because they were not held by police. Such an inspection could have yielded additional information that would have been helpful in reaching a conclusion in this case.

(11) A suggestion that there is information that the officer did not have as a result of not inspecting the vehicles, by the attack, "Wouldn't you have liked to have seen the vehicles?"

(12) The officer was not able to recreate the exact weather conditions for visibility assessment tests.

Comment. These tests provided the basis for the officer's opinion that the defendant had enough time to take a successful evasion action. The faulty tests therefore lead to a faulty conclusion about negligence or culpability.

(13) The visibility assessment tests did not accurately reproduce the conditions at the time of the accident.

Comment. This means that the alignment of the headlights, the height of the headlights, the model and power of the lamps, etc., may have been different; the weather, phase of the moon, etc., could have been different than on the night of the accident. This cross-examination can be drawn out, and inoculation is called for if such tests did, in fact, differ from the actual conditions at the time of the crash. A good defense attorney may try to suppress the results of the tests by submitting a pretrial motion, and such a motion may be successful.

(14) The visibility assessment was made by an alerted operator and therefore yielded an unnatural, inaccurate result.

Comment. There is no reason to believe that the defendant should have been alerted to the possible presence of a dangerous situation on the night of the accident and therefore would have had less visibility of such a danger.

(15) The drag sled used by the police weighs only ___ lbs., and therefore does not accurately measure the friction produced by a car that weighs more than a hundred times as much. The drag sled does not accurately reproduce the effects of tire pressure, temperature, weight shift, etc. that a car would have associated with its ability to stop. These attacks are not consistent with validation studies that show the drag sled does produce acceptable measurements of the road friction. (1,2)

(16) The officer only measured the drag factor in one place, and the road may have had inconsistencies or differences over the length of the skid pattern that was analyzed to determine the speed of the defendant's vehicle. Such differences were not taken into account, and therefore the speed estimate is too high.

(17) The officer did not take into account the weight distribution on the four wheels of the vehicle, but instead, averaged the four skid mark lengths together as though the weight was distributed equally on all four wheels. A specification sheet for the vehicle shows this is not the case, and this error taints the accuracy of the analysis and the results.

(18) The overlapping tire marks were incorrectly analyzed. Since the back tires were sliding over marks already left by the front tires, the drag factor measured on the unmarked road surface should not have been applied to the rear skid marks. This failure to account for the presence of the front tire marks when the rear tire marks were made yields the wrong drag factor and the wrong result in the calculations.

(19) The defendant's vehicle has anti-lock brakes, but that was not considered in the calculations. By not doing so the wrong drag factor was used in the calculations.

(20) The scale that was used to pull the drag sled was not calibrated, so its accuracy is in question. That scale reading was used to calculate the drag factor,

which in turn was used to estimate the speed of the defendant's vehicle, and therefore the accuracy of the scale is directly related to the accuracy of the speed estimate.

Comment. While this seems like a logical argument, a sensitivity analysis using a range of drag factors that reflect possible uncertainties in the drag factor, would have shown the result to not be significantly dependent upon the accuracy of the drag sled measurement.

(21) There was a significant time passed between the time of the accident and the time that drag factor tests were done, making the tests undependable.

Comment. This is not a valid attack, unless the road surface conditions had changed significantly in that time. One attack, when there is rain, suggests that as more and more rain falls on the road surface, oil is brought up from the asphalt surface, causing a lubrication effect and significantly changing the drag factor of the road surface. Drag sled measurements are not recommended on wet road surfaces.

(22) Other drag factor attacks include:

(a) Tire tread difference between the tires on the vehicle and the tread on the drag sled;
(b) Failure to adjust the drag factor for speeds above 30 mph;
(c) The sled jerks when it is pulled, yielding large errors in reading the scale used to pull the sled (this is not a valid attack, because the scale is read only when it is smooth, and not "bouncing");
(d) Each individual car has different braking performance, and the use of a single number for the road surface applied to all vehicles is inaccurate (the attorney may use braking test results from *Popular Science* or some other magazine to show this, but such comparative tests are often done on different surfaces, with different brake pedal pressure, etc.);
(e) Drag sleds are not accepted by engineers or experts in the field of accident reconstructionists;
(f) Errors made in the measurements of drag factor and skid mark lengths are cumulative and can produce large errors when calculations are done;
(g) There is a certain skill involved in using a drag sled to avoid bouncing and the jerking motion that results when the sled first breaks lose from the surface and starts to slide (in some cases the defense attorney will have the officer demonstrate the use of the sled to show this to the jury);

(h) The appearance of the sled and the scale used to pull it are not very scientific, and the results of measurements with the sled should be suspect;

(i) If an accelerometer (VC 2000, G-Analyst, etc.) was used to measure the drag factor, it is an electronic "black box," and the officer has no way of checking whether it is measuring correctly;

(j) The officer does not even know how the accelerometer works; or

(k) The officer has not calibrated the accelerometer against another method for measuring the drag factor, and therefore does not know if it is accurate.

(23) Attacks on the speed estimate from skid marks might also include:

(a) A skid test using an exemplar vehicle was used to measure the drag factor, not the defendant's vehicle;

(b) The differences in the lengths of the skid marks indicates the possibility of some problem with the braking system of the defendant's vehicle — a problem that would not have been apparent unless an emergency situation occurred;

(c) The defendant says, "The car felt funny when I hit the brakes — it just seemed to slide, and I couldn't keep control of it";

(d) The skid marks went from left to right, and the drag factor was different on different lateral location on the road because of road wear; failure to take this into account means the wrong drag factor was used in the calculations;

(e) The defendant's vehicle was rotating during the skid, and the failure to include such rotation led to a significant error in the speed estimate (if the brakes were locked during the rotation, there is no need to account for the rotation within the calculations); or

(f) Wetting the road with a fire hose does not produce the same lubrication as a gentle, soaking rain would have on the day of the accident — this yields a drag factor that is too high.

§ 4-9(c). Errors in Investigation or Reconstruction.

(1) Do you consider a certain book to be authoritative? (Note: The examiner is trying to use a book to impeach your testimony and has chosen a specific section, paragraph, or sentence from the book which he/she believes will contradict your prior testimony.)

Q. Officer, you testified earlier that your calculations included the radius of the yaw marks that the defendant's vehicle made on the road?

A. That's correct. I measured the chord and middle ordinate of the marks to determine the radius of the yaw.

Q. And it was your testimony that you used that radius to find the speed of the defendant's vehicle. Is that correct?

A. Yes.

Q. Are you familiar with the book by _____ on accident reconstruction that I have in my hand?

A. Yes.

Q. Have you ever used this book?

A. Yes.

Q. Do you consider it to be an authoritative source in the field of accident reconstruction?

A. Yes.

Q. I'd like you to look at page ___, and read to yourself the portion that I marked. Doesn't the author of that book say that the correct radius to use in yaw calculations is the radius curve made by the center of mass of the vehicle?

A. Yes.

Q. But that isn't what you used in your calculations, is it?

A. No.

Comment. The officer got into trouble by acknowledging the text to be "authoritative." The witness should have asked to see the section of the text the examiner was interested in before accepting the entire book as authoritative. This strategy should be identified by the witness as an impending attempt to impeach prior testimony. A more correct answer might have been, "Are you asking about a specific part of the book?" or "Can I see the part of the book that you're interested in?" or "I wouldn't say that I agree with everything in the book without looking at whatever section you're referring to." And the answer to the final question might be, "No, but may I explain?"

(2) There were portions of the defendant's vehicle motion where no tire marks were observed, and in these parts of the motion the car was rolling, not sliding. The assumption should have been that the vehicle was rolling during these parts of the motion, and that a rolling drag factor (approximately .02-.03) should have

been used for these parts of the motion. The officer did not use a rolling drag factor, and therefore the calculations are too high.

> Q. Officer, you stated in your direct testimony that there were areas where no tire marks were observed?
>
> A. Yes, that's correct.
>
> Q. And you said that the lack of tire mark evidence was because the tires "just didn't mark some of the time." Isn't that what you said?
>
> A. Yes.
>
> Q. Couldn't the lack of tire marks have been because the tires were rolling at those times, and didn't leave any mark because of that?
>
> A. That was not what I concluded.
>
> Q. Can you tell the jury what the road would look like if a tire rolled over it? Would there be any kind of a mark made by the tire?
>
> A. No.
>
> Q. So you'd have to agree with me that when there is no mark it could be because the tire was rolling at that point?
>
> A. Yes, I guess so.
>
> Q. If a tire is rolling, you're aware of the fact that the friction is much lower than it would be if the tire were locked up and sliding, aren't you?
>
> A. Yes.
>
> Q. And that would be represented by using a very low drag factor for the rolling tire, say .02 to .03, wouldn't it?
>
> A. Yes.
>
> Q. And if you used a drag factor of .02, that would be 40 times less than the drag factor you used for your calculations in this case, wouldn't it?
>
> A. Yes.

Comment. A skilled cross-examiner would probably not go any further with this question string, but would argue at the end of the case that the officer's own testimony was that the wrong drag factor was used, and the speed estimate would therefore be much too high. The officer has to alert the jury and the prosecutor to the fact that only a small portion of the tire pattern was missing, and that a lower drag factor (for rolling tires) applied to such a small part of the tire pattern would not have significantly changed the speed estimate. An answer such as, "yes, but may I explain" could have been used to interrupt the flow of the defense attorney's logic.

(3) The officer did not know exactly how the defendant's vehicle got to the final rest position, and therefore the post-impact analysis was incorrect or based on a faulty assumption.

Q. You stated in your earlier testimony that my client's vehicle moved after the impact?

A. Yes.

Q. And you said you analyzed that part of the motion and included it in your speed estimate before the impact?

A. Yes, that's correct.

Q. You'd agree with me, wouldn't you, that if you made a mistake in analyzing the post-impact motion of my client's vehicle, it would cause a mistake in the pre-impact estimate of speed as well?

A. Yes, I guess so, but I don't know by how much.

Q. But you'd agree that there would be a mistake in the pre-impact speed estimate that you testified to earlier in your direct examination testimony?

A. Yes.

Q. Was there any evidence of exactly how my client's vehicle moved after separating form the impact?

A. There was some evidence, but not for the whole path of the motion.

Q. Then the answer to my question is no. Is that correct?

A. Yes.

Q. In fact, your report doesn't say much about the post-impact motion of my client's vehicle, does it?

A. No.

Q. And there are no photographs of any tire marks made by my client's vehicle after it separated from the impact, are there?

A. No.

Q. So, as you sit here today, you can't tell the jury exactly how my client's vehicle separated from the collision, what exact angle it was heading, how many degrees it rotated, whether all the brakes were applied, how much braking pressure my client was using, or anything else about how it reached its final rest position?

A. That's correct.

Comment. The attorney might then continue the attack, or wait to argue the implied error in the post-impact motion analysis during the final argument of the trial. The witness should alert the prosecutor that he/she wants to clear up this matter on redirect, by answering "yes, but may I explain" during the testimony.

Attacks on the Police Witness' Credibility.

(4) The witness did not review all materials before reaching conclusions. (Note: This attack may often be available because additional information is developed, including discovery of the defense expert's work, after the prosecution's reconstructionist or toxicologist has reached an opinion. This is most effectively dealt with during the inoculation within the direct examination of the witness.)

Q. You submitted your report in this case on June 14, 1998. Is that correct?

A. Yes.

Q. And at the time you based your opinions in that report on everything you had reviewed and all the work you had done personally in this case up to that time?

A. Yes.

Q. You'd agree with me, wouldn't you, that if additional information was available after you completed your report, you would have to review and reconcile that information with opinions expressed in your earlier report?

A. Well, that depends. (Note: This is a good answer, because it shows that your opinion would not necessarily change as a result of seeing additional information.)

Q. You're aware, aren't you, of information today, that you didn't have when you reached your conclusions and wrote your official report in this case?

A. Yes.

Q. You didn't submit any addendum or supplemental report in this case, did you?

A. No.

Q. So you reached your opinion before you had all the information that was available in this case?

A. The additional information didn't change anything for me.

Comment. The police witness has informed the jury that additional information did not negate his/her original opinion(s) in the case. This attack could have been superseded by inoculation during the direct examination.

(5) The witness' experience, although having worked on hundreds of cases, can be whittled down when compared to this specific fact pattern.

Q. You stated in your earlier testimony that you investigated and/or reconstructed over 300 accidents prior to the particular one we are here about today?

A. Yes.

Q. Of those 300 plus accidents, how many occurred at night?

A. About 75 or so.

Q. And of those "75 or so," how many involved two vehicles approaching each other like the two cars in this case?

A. Maybe 20 or so.

Q. And of those "20 or so" that were similar to the accident in this case, how many involved pre-impact braking by both vehicles involved in the accident?

A. Five or six.

Q. And of those "five or six" accidents similar to the one involving my client, how many of them involved two vehicles like the ones involved in this accident?

A. None.

Q. So although you have a lot of experience in other kinds of cases, the fact is that you have never before investigated or reconstructed an accident in which the facts were the same as in this case?

A. When you say it that way, I guess I'd have to say yes.

Comment. Rarely will the last question be asked in an actual case. Most competent defense counsel will ask the question and give the answer himself or herself in their final argument to the jury. This diminishing of the officer's experience by narrowing down to the specific facts in a particular case is always a way of attacking the witness, but it is done with some risk to the credibility of the defense attorney. The jury is wise enough to know that there is no need for the witness to have experience in the exact type of case, and this sort of attack may backfire on the cross-examiner.

(6) Additional attacks on the credibility of the police witness might include:

    (a) The witness changed his/her report after seeing the report of the defense expert in the case;

    (b) Did you do any video taping at the scene? — Where is the video?;

    (c) The witness has never done similar tests in other cases, and did not have an experienced officer assist with the tests in this case;

    (d) The witness has not published papers or participated in any tests or studies that some of the other police officers in the department have;

    (e) The officer did not consult with anyone else on this case, or have anyone check over his/her work (there may be an error that the witness has not detected in the analysis);

    (f) The witness did not personally inspect the defendant's vehicle for mechanical defects and is not qualified to do so;

    (g) The witness has no formal training in physics, which is the foundation for the calculations he/she used to reach opinion(s) in this case;

    (h) The police investigator did not show the locations of civilian witnesses on the scale drawing of the scene;

    (i) The police witness did not measure and document witness locations as part of his/her investigation;

    (j) The witness did not repeat measurements to be sure that an error had not been made;

    (k) The investigator did not return to the scene of a night crash to look for additional evidence during the daytime (the witness would probably have to agree that some forms of evidence would not be very visible at nighttime, but would be more observable in daylight);

    (l) The officer did not take photographs showing the witness' perspective;

    (m) The investigator did not re-interview an important witness in the case; or

    (n) The officer did not interview the witness with the witness located where the observations were made.

§ 4-9(d). Attacks on the Certainty of Opinion(s).

(1) The witness did not do a sensitivity analysis to confirm the certainty of the calculated speed estimates. (Note: A sensitivity analysis should be done in every case where there is any doubt about the effect that different input information

would have on the results of the calculations. In some cases the officer knows from experience that the calculation is not significantly sensitive to the input information, but it is not a bad idea to do the sensitivity analysis just to be sure.)

Q. You testified earlier that your opinion of the speed of my client's vehicle was that he was traveling at a minimum of 56 mph at the start of the skid marks?

A. Yes.

Q. You weren't able to determine an exact speed?

A. No.

Q. And in estimating the speed of my client's vehicle you used a measurement of that pulling force on the sled?

A. Yes.

Q. And the weight of the drag sled itself was part of the calculation?

A. Yes.

Q. And each of the four skid marks was measured and used in your calculation, weren't they?

A. Yes.

Q. And there was some number 30 that you said was a "constant"?

A. Yes.

Q. In fact, it isn't exactly 30, is it?

A. It's real close to 30, that's what we were trained to put into the equation.

Q. The fact is that each of your measurements — all six of them — and the number 30 in the equation — they could all be a little different than the numbers you used?

A. I guess so, but I don't think they could be very different.

Q. If all six of the numbers that went into your calculation were different, the answer that you got when you used your calculator would, of course, be different, wouldn't it?

A. To some extent.

Comment. The witness should not leave the jury with the conception that the speed estimate is anything but a minimum. If the testimony is left as it now stands the defense attorney might argue successfully later that the calculation is simply wrong. By the witness talking about a sensitivity analysis, the certainty of the speed estimate should be established in the jurors' minds.

(2) The point of impact is uncertain — no scuff marks, no debris pattern, no jog, no evidence of pre-impact movement of the pedestrian or bicyclist is known.

Q. Officer, you testified earlier that you were not able to determine an exact point of impact in this pedestrian case. Isn't that correct?

A. Yes, I was only able to determine a probable impact area.

Q. And that's because there was no evidence from the tires of my client's car to show where the accident occurred?

A. That's right.

Q. And there was no evidence from the shoes of the pedestrian to show where the accident occurred?

A. That's right.

Q. And the witnesses in the case were not able to pinpoint exactly where the pedestrian was when the accident occurred?

A. That's correct.

Q. One way of determining the speed of my client's vehicle in a case like this is to use the distance the pedestrian's body moved to find the speed of the car, isn't that true?

A. Yes.

Q. And of course, without knowing where the point of impact was, you couldn't use that method in this case, could you?

A. No.

Q. And you're familiar with a term called "projection efficiency" as it is applied to a car striking a pedestrian?

A. Yes.

Q. And the use of that information would require that you know where the point of impact was, wouldn't it?

A. Yes.

Q. So in this case you couldn't use the projection efficiency concept to do any calculations, could you?

A. No.

Q. And isn't there a technique for estimating vehicle speed that includes the distance a body slides on the ground and the total "throw distance" of the pedestrian's body to find the speed of the car?

A. Yes.

Q. But without knowing the point of impact you couldn't do that calculation?

A. No, there wasn't enough information to do that type of calculation.

Q. Wouldn't you have liked to have been able to do some other type of calculation to corroborate the speed estimate that you made from the tire marks?

A. That would have been nice, but there wasn't enough information to do that in this case.

Q. So of the four or five ways that you might have determined the speed of my client's vehicle, you were able to use only one method. And you could not confirm that estimate with a second calculation, could you?

A. No.

Comment. The defense attorney has implied an uncertainty to the jury in this case in which there was not enough evidence to do any additional calculations. The witness must be convincing and persuasive during the direct testimony about the speed estimate, and may have addressed the lack of evidence during the inoculation phase of the direct examination.

When two vehicles (or a vehicle and an object) make initial contact, the location where first contact occurs is called the point of impact (POI). In some cases the POI cannot be determined precisely and an "area of impact" is reported. The point of impact may be an important factor in establishing culpability, especially in cases where a vehicle has crossed the center line, or in pedestrian collisions. When vehicles engage, tremendous impact forces can act on the vehicles, causing sudden changes in the direction and/or speed of the vehicles. In such cases there may be physical evidence of these impact forces, including:

- Change in direction of pre-impact skid marks (called "jogs" or "offsets");
- Gouges or scrapes on the pavement made by the vehicle undercarriage;
- Fluid spills and fluid throw patterns;
- Impact scuffmarks from tires that suddenly change direction;
- Debris from the impact; or
- Paint transferred to the pavement.

Whenever evidence of the point of impact is observed it should be matched to the vehicle that caused it as specifically as possible. For example, a gouge in the road should be matched to the part of the vehicle that caused it by looking under the vehicle for fresh scratches, broken parts of the suspension, road material sticking to the undercarriage of the vehicle, etc. This type of evidence is sometimes poorly documented by an investigator who reaches a quick conclusion about the point of impact without considering how that conclusion might be challenged later or how accurately the POI can be determined. Photographs of the evidence and field notes about the appearance of the evidence can be very helpful when the POI is brought into question later. The point of impact should be corroborated by witnesses, drivers, or passengers in the vehicle to whatever extent is possible. When the POI is correlated to the pre-impact path of the vehicle, the nature of any evasive actions by either driver might be determined.

(3) The police report did not include any mention of the fact that the defendant's car had ABS brakes.

Comment. The documentation of any "ABS scuff marks" or photographs of ABS tire marks should be part of the police report if the braking analysis is being used to estimate the defendant's speed. If this seems to be an issue that is expected at trial, the witness should be sure the prosecutor understands any differences between ABS and conventional braking that might come up at trial.

(4) A motorcycle rear-only skid mark was observed at the scene, and no front braking was assumed.

Comment. A range of braking for the front wheel should be used in a sensitivity analysis to see what effect it might have on the ultimate opinion of causation in the case. This is an area where the testimony of the motorcycle operator is really the only source of information.

(5) The witness made an assumption as part of the calculations. (Note: How is the opinion affected if a different assumption is made, how reliable or probable is it that the assumption is valid, and was a range of values assumed for a particular calculation?)

    Q.   Let's look at your estimate of the speed of my client's vehicle. You said you assumed full braking for all four tires of the car when you did your reconstruction?

    A.   Yes, I did.

    Q.   But, in fact, the skid marks from the four tires were not all the same length, were they?

A. No, they were slightly different.

Q. You didn't consider that the lengths of the marks were different because of some unbalanced braking, did you?

A. No.

Q. And if you had considered that you might have come up with a different answer in your calculations?

A. I don't think so.

Q. But you didn't even consider that possibility, even though the tire marks made when the brakes were applied were different lengths?

A. No I didn't.

Comment. The officer, based on prior knowledge, training, and experience, observed the skid marks and concluded that there was no unbalanced braking, so he/she should not be satisfied with leaving an impression of that possibility with the jurors. Perhaps a statement like, "all the brakes were working, because there were four distinct marks — one from each wheel of the car," would have been more appropriate.

(6) The defense attorney suggests the possibility of an error in the calculations. (Note: This can be a risky attack, especially if the prosecutor uses redirect examination to address the implied error and shows there was none. The logic of this attack appeals to the juror's own experiences, though, and its potential effectiveness should not be underestimated if the witness' credibility has been damaged by other elements of the cross-examination.)

Q. Officer, have you ever made a mistake in a calculation, and then found the mistake when you looked over your work at a later time?

A. Yes.

Q. And I'm sure you've had the experience that I've had that I looked at something that was wrong again and again and a mistake in it just didn't register until someone else looked at it, and then it jumped out for the other person?

A. Yes, that's happened to me.

Q. Have you ever had the experience of finding a mistake in time to correct it or to make a supplemental report of it?

A. I don't think that's happened to me.

Q. But you'd agree that it's possible to make a mistake and not even recognize it when you look over your work yourself?

A. I guess so.

Q. How do you know that hasn't happened in this case?

A. I reviewed my calculations, and I didn't find any mistake.

Comment. This attack can be set up during the opening statement, or by earlier questions in the cross-examination that attack the expertise and/or formal training of the witness. The witness can avoid this implication by having another officer, or a supervisor, check his/her work. It sounds much more professional to have had someone check all calculations as a matter of policy or ordinary procedure.

The best thing for the witness to remember is that he/she controls time. The witness should never be in a hurry to answer a question — it does not improve credibility to answer quickly, and it may even open the door for more strenuous cross-examination if something is misstated. Once an answer is given, the witness cannot change it or edit it without his/her credibility being damaged.

References

(1) Bruce D. Wakefield, James E. Cothem, Ronald Sellers, and Gregory Carver, "Roadway Drag Factor Determination, Dynamic v. Static," N.A.T.A.R.I. newsletter, Fourth Quarter, 1995.

(2) John Kwasnoski, "Drag Sled Measurements Yield Valid Minimum Speed Estimates," N.A.T.A.R.I. newsletter, Third Quarter, 1998.

Appendix A

ACCIDENT RECONSTRUCTION ASSOCIATIONS

The telephone numbers of the associations have not been included since they frequently change; to receive additional information about how to contact any of the associations, two national resources are cited at the beginning of the list.

Accreditation Commission for Traffic Accident Reconstuctionists (ACTAR)
800-799-8384

American Prosecutors Research Institute (APRI)
703-549-4253

Association for the Advancement of Automotive Medicine (AAAM)

Canadian Association of Technical Accident Investigators and Reconstructionists (CATAIR)

Forensic Accident Reconstructionists of Oregon (FARO)

Illinois Association of Technical Accident Investigators (IATAI)

International Association of Accident Reconstruction Specialists

Maryland Association of Traffic Accident Investigators (MdATAI)

Midwestern Association of Technical Accident Investigators (MwATAI)

National Association of Professional Accident Reconstruction Specialists (NAPARS)

National Association of Technical Accident Reconstructionists and Investigators (NATARI)

New Jersey Association of Accident Reconstructionists (NJAAR)

Society of Automotive Engineers (SAE)

Society of Accident Reconstructionists (SOAR)

Southwestern Association of Traffic Accident Investigators (SATAI)

Texas Association of Accident Reconstruction Specialists (TAARS)

Washington Association of Traffic Accident Investigators (WATAI)

Appendix B

COMPUTER-GENERATED EVIDENCE

The rapid advancement in computer technology has made the cost of software packages fall at a dramatic rate, and reconstruction, simulation, and even animation software that cost tens of thousands of dollars just a few years ago is now available and is being used more frequently by experts. The output of these software packages includes slick graphics, time-lapse drawings of the collision dynamics, spreadsheets of data and calculations, and the capability to transform the graphics directly into video animations. While the output product may look intimidating to prosecutors unfamiliar with such evidence, nonetheless, it is a necessity that at some point a prosecutor will have to evaluate such evidence and cross examine an expert who has relied on the software to give opinion testimony. This is a case where detailed preparation is absolutely a must, and where conferencing with the state's expert is a necessity.

A description of the types of software is included below, followed by a section on attacking computer-assisted reconstruction testimony which will give the prosecutor some guidelines and suggestions to use as a starting point.

Computer-Assisted Reconstruction Software

Accident reconstruction softwares can be broken down into several types based on the function they perform or the level of sophistication of the calculations. These types include:

- simple calculations (similar to those done on a calculator);
- computer-aided drawing (including surveying capabilities);
- photogrammetry (measurements made from photographs);
- reconstruction of pre-impact motions from evidence;
- simulation of vehicle motions from given pre-impact conditions; and
- animations (production of a video of the vehicle motions).

Simple calculations. These software packages, costing less than fifty dollars and sometimes free of charge as "shareware," perform the same functions as using a handheld calculator. The convenience of being able to respond to on-screen requests for input data and the apparent authoritative appearance of the output seem to be the main reasons why these packages have become so prolific. In reality, the computer calculation adds no credibility or accuracy to the calculation since the software is just doing algebraic and trigonometric calculations at the simplest level in most cases. The results from the software can easily be checked with a hand calculator.

> **Trial Tip**
>
> *The police witness should disclose to the jury that calculations done on a computer are just quicker than those done by calculator. This willingness to inform the jury about the relative value of these two methods of calculating can enhance the witness' credibility by establishing the honesty of the police witness.*

Computer-Aided Drawing. The use of computer programs and laser printers to make drawings has been given the name Computer-Aided Drawing (CAD). Older software (and/or the limitation of using a dot matrix printer) produces choppy, segmented drawings that do not have smooth curves as part of the drawing capability. These drawings, although made "to scale," do not have the fine detail that may be available with more expensive software, do not have vehicle icons that look real, and may not have the ability to draw irregular-shaped objects, trees, curved tire marks, etc. More recent software, on the other hand, includes a library of "clip art" icons for cars, motorcycles, tractor-trailers, etc. and many of the common scene components such as sewer grates, traffic signs, etc. that produce more realistic drawings of crash scenes. Curbing can be drawn with the proper radii (curvature), making the drawings look clear, sharp, and very professional. The use of CAD software has given a more polished appearance to accident reconstruction reports, but the reviewer should remember that the drawings contain no more accurate information than a well-drawn site drawing made with conventional drafting tools.

In some of the CAD software, the user has the ability to produce three-dimensional drawings of the results, and these drawings can be made from user-selected perspectives within the drawing. This gives the user the ability to look at the drawing from the position of witnesses, operators, and vehicle occupants, and can be helpful in acquiring information from witnesses by using the animation to check or enhance their recollections of what they observed.

A variation of this procedure is to use a computerized transit at the scene to record evidence locations on a diskette, which is then downloaded into software that can make a scale drawing of the site measurements, completely replacing the use of measuring tapes or wheels and the recording of evidence in field notes that must later be plotted by hand to construct site drawings. Several such systems are currently available and their accuracy has been verified in tests and has been reported in reconstruction literature and by the manufacturers. One obvious advantage of such measuring-drawing systems is the elimination of errors made in recording and/or transposing numerical measurements in the drawing process.

APPENDIX B

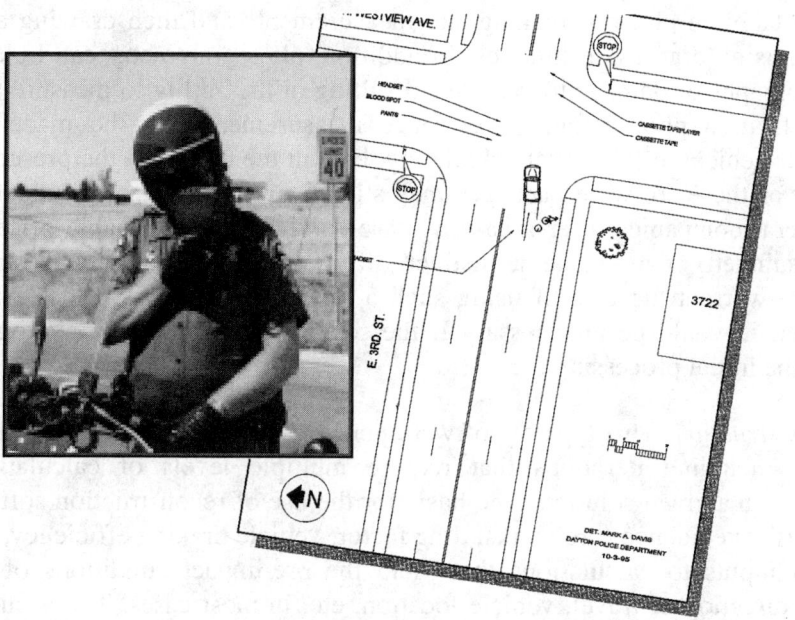

Courtesy of Laser Technology, Inc. (www.lasertech.com)

Trial Tip

A computer-generated drawing can be taken back to the scene to make some comparison measurements — this verifies that the drawing is to scale, and that the electronic surveying equipment was working correctly.

Photogrammetry. Photogrammetry is the science of making measurements from photographic images. This requires a scanner to scan the photograph into the computer software, and also requires measurements of several reference points within the photograph to be used by the software to make measurements of other dimensions within the picture. These software can be invaluable in extracting evidence such as the locations of tire marks, gouges, final rest positions of vehicles, etc., that were not measured by the investigating officer at the time the scene was processed. The user typically scans the photograph onto the screen of the computer, then clicks on points of interest within the photograph, and by using menu selections is then able to measure the various evidence locations to produce coordinates of the evidence, measure distances between two evidence locations, determine the angle between two lines, or produce a two-dimensional drawing of the scene from the photograph. This last function can actually take the place of making site measurements and then drawing a scene diagram using drafting techniques. In addition, photogrammetry can be applied to photographs of damage to vehicles, resulting in the ability to measure a crash profile from a photograph, if reference measurements can be made on an exemplar vehicle or the actual vehicle involved in the crash. At the present time, the cost of these software packages may still be prohibitive to individual users, but several companies offer a case-by-case service at a reasonable price. Such photogrammetry may make a distinct difference in an individual case and therefore warrant the cost of using such a procedure to retrieve lost evidence. However, it would be unnecessary if the scene were completely photographed during the initial processing.

Reconstruction. This type of software performs calculations that may be very tedious, including iterations that require multiple levels of calculations to converge on a given solution. The basis for the use of reconstruction software is that physical evidence (tire marks, drag factor, vehicle braking efficiency, etc.) is used as inputs to calculations that yield the pre-impact conditions of speed, vehicle direction of travel, vehicle location, etc. in most cases. The accuracy of the reconstruction depends to a great extent on the accuracy and detail of the physical evidence collected at the scene; in cases where evidence is not available, the user is forced to call upon a database within the software for "default" values to be used in lieu of measured evidence or vehicle parameters. Many reconstruction softwares include the capacity to print out a time-lapse graphic of the vehicle motions or a three-dimensional drawing of vehicle positions. Some also have the ability to produce a video animation directly from the reconstruction software.

Simulation. These softwares enable the user to input the vehicle data, pre-impact vehicle locations, directions and speeds of the vehicles and other parameters, and have the software simulate how the vehicles would engage and their post-impact motions to final rest positions. The software may also have the option of showing the tire markings that would be produced, the vehicle damage profiles, and other post-impact details of the crash. A common use of simulation software is to check reconstructed vehicle speeds by determining whether reconstructed pre-impact conditions of motion would produce the post-impact evidence that was observed by investigators. This software allows "what if" scenarios to check on alternative vehicle speeds that may be opined by the defendant's expert. If the defendant's pre-impact speeds will not produce the observed post-impact evidence this can be used to discredit the expert's reconstruction opinions. The simulation software usually allows the user to enter driver activity such as braking and steering inputs during the crash, and these are sometimes speculative or based on user assumptions. The vehicle database within the software can usually be customized to reflect inertial properties of the actual vehicles involved in the crash so that default vehicle parameters do not have to be used. In effect, the simulation software asks the user "How did the vehicles approach each other?" and then shows the user how the vehicle would have moved during and after engagement.

Animation. These software require large amounts of computer capacity compared to other software types, and can produce animated drawings directly onto videotape from either a reconstruction or simulation software package or from direct input of parameters by the user. The result may be either a very realistic video of the vehicle motions, including the crash environment (buildings, trees, etc.), or a less-finished look in which vehicles are rectangular, detail in the environment is missing, and/or the vehicle motions are choppy. The animation can usually be generated from various perspective locations, which gives the user a wide range of uses for the finished product. A variation of the animation technique involves using an actual photograph of the crash scene and then animating the vehicle icons into the scene photograph, which gives the animation a very realistic appearance.

Admissibility Considerations. A basic consideration for the prosecutor is whether the computer-assisted evidence will be offered as demonstrative evidence or substantive evidence at trial. The admissibility of the results of calculation or CAD software should be relatively easy to deal with. On the other hand, the more sophisticated software for reconstruction, simulation, and animation may be more readily challenged. The use of the computer-generated animation as a chalk that an expert uses to demonstrate his/her reconstruction testimony may relieve much of the burden of admissibility. Some of the more frequently cited admissibility considerations include :

- failure to warn opposition of intent to use animation and to disclose the technical contents of the software, including program listing;
- evidence is redundant or repetitive;
- computer-assisted evidence is prejudicial rather than probative (by its form it can have an effect which goes beyond its ostensible use);
- calculations are beyond the capability of the witness;
- the computer results cannot be verified by the user as being accurate (in effect, the user has employed the software as a "black box" into which input evidence or assumptions have been blindly fed);
- input information may not be in evidence;
- software documentation (list of how the program calculates) was not made available to opposition prior to trial;

- the animation should be based on the results of reconstruction calculations and should not be "created" by the animator by placing vehicles at points or at speeds determined by the animator or attorney;
- lack of input information requires "default" values selected within the software which do not match evidence in the crash;
- judges may not understand the technology and therefore misinterpret the computer-generated results;
- use of computer-generated results does not satisfy the Frye criteria;
- lack of appropriate foundation — user made assumptions that are interpreted by the software as physical evidence upon which reconstructions or simulations are based;
- software was misapplied to a scenario for which the software was not designed (many reconstruction and simulation softwares require a plane surface and will not accurately handle differences in elevation such as ditches, off-road movements, grades or superelevations);
- mischaracterizing an animation as "the way it was" rather than as a depiction of the witness' opinion; and
- failure to present testimony regarding the "real time" nature of an animation or the fact that the animation is done to a true scale.

An excellent (although not very recent) reference to these software types is an S.A.E. paper by Thomas Bohan (1). Additional information on computer-generated evidence can be found in the literature (2,3,4,5,6). The National Traffic Law Center also maintains files on computer-aided evidence and current court decisions regarding admissibility.

References

(1) Thomas L. Bohan, Computer-Aided Accident Reconstruction: Its Role in Court, S.A.E. # 910370.

(2) Richard J. Fay, Computer Images and Animations in Court, S.A.E. #970965.

(3) Terry D. Day and Randall L. Hargens, Application and Misapplication of Computer Programs for Accident Reconstruction, S.A.E. #890738.

(4) Ian S. Jones, David W. Muir, and Stephen W. Groo, Computer Animation — Admissibility in the Courtroom, S.A.E. #910366.

(5) Accident Reconstruction: Technology and Animation VII, S.A.E. # SP-1237.

(6) Accident Reconstruction: Technology and Animation III, S.A.E. # SP-946.

Appendix C

IMPAIRMENT AT LOW BLOOD ALCOHOL CONCENTRATIONS

Driving Skills Associated with Observations that Trigger the Traffic Stop

The following driving skills are first measurably impaired at the BAC level shown to the right of each skill description. These skills are more completely described in connection with specific crash scenarios, and the scientific articles defining the tests are referenced in Low BAC Driver Impairment, published by Legal Sciences, Inc., and available at www.legalsciences.com.

Driving Skill	First Measurable Impairment
simple reaction time Time from decision to the onset of the reaction response.	.03
choice reaction time errors Subject makes errors in selecting the appropriate response from a number of options available.	.05
pursuit tracking Operator must keep vehicle within marked lanes as his/her vehicle follows another moving vehicle, or must keep his/her vehicle aligned behind the leading vehicle.	.02
tracking Ability to keep vehicle on traveled part of road and avoid swerving across fog line or crossing the center line or into another lane of travel.	.03
concentrated attention Ability to focus on roadway and maintain vigilance and forward gaze.	.07
divided attention — detection of/ response to peripheral stimuli Ability of operator to detect stimuli outside the central field of vision (peripheral view) while performing another task or processing information.	.02
visual search Ability to maintain searching pattern for objects on or about the roadway.	.05

interpretation of signals .05
Ability of the operator to interpret brake lights, traffic signals, etc. is impaired, even though the operator perceives the signal.

comprehension .05
Subject cannot accurately comprehend what has been perceived, and may misinterpret stimulus or be unable to process the information.

visual information processing .06
Recognition and decision-making ability, using visual information.

information processing rate .07
Time to process from the point of perception to the point of recognition.

double vision, other vision impairment .05
Ability to focus and perceive an image clearly, thus affecting recognition of an object as being in a dangerous position.

depth perception .08
Ability to determine distance between subject (and subject's vehicle) and object being perceived.

peripheral vision with central task .04
Limited peripheral vision when driver is making driving decisions.

time perception .04
Subject has a distorted perception of time, and may feel that situation is occurring in slow motion, or may portray a distorted perception of time in describing a situation.

coordination .02
Motor coordination is impaired.

motor performance .06
Ability to perform motor tasks, movements, and other reactions.

vehicle alignment .03
Vehicle suddenly tracks off roadway, crosses fog or center line, or is driving in breakdown lane.

impaired tracking, steering, braking, gear changing .03
Basic driving skills are impaired.

APPENDIX C

spatial judgment, impaired driving skills .04
   Ability to judge space between vehicles, or vehicle and object
   is impaired, and general driving skills are impaired to some extent.

curve negotiating .05
   Operator cannot steer around curve, or is impaired in ability to judge
   steering, speed, etc. to successfully negotiate a curve in the roadway.

speed changes .07
   Operator cannot adjust to speed changes or make appropriate
   speed changes in his/her vehicle in response to driving demands.

lateral position error, steering correction time .07
   Driver operates in the wrong lane, or in breakdown lane; time is
   lengthened to realign the vehicle in response to a stimulus.

Appendix D

IMPAIRMENT AT LOW BLOOD ALCOHOL CONCENTRATIONS

Skills Associated with Observations During Field Sobriety Tests

The following skills that result in observations during the SFST's are first measurably impaired at the BAC level shown to the right of each skill description. These skills are more completely described in connection with specific crash scenarios, and the scientific articles defining the tests are referenced in Low BAC Driver Impairment, published by Legal Sciences, Inc., and available at www.legalsciences.com.

Driving Skill	First Measurable Impairment
simple reaction time Time from decision to the onset of the reaction response.	.03
choice reaction time errors Subject makes errors in selecting the appropriate response from a number of options available.	.05
concentrated attention Ability to focus on roadway and maintain vigilance and forward gaze.	.07
visual recognition Ability to recognize objects after they have been perceived.	.07
comprehension Subject cannot accurately comprehend what has been perceived, and may misinterpret stimulus or be unable to process the information.	.05
visual information processing Recognition and decision-making ability, using visual information.	.06
information processing rate Time to process from the point of perception to the point of recognition.	.07
double vision, other vision impairment Ability to focus and perceive an image clearly, thus affecting recognition of an object as being in a dangerous position.	.05

depth perception .08
Ability to determine distance between subject (and subject's vehicle) and object being perceived.

time perception .04
Subject has a distorted perception of time, and may feel that situation is occurring in slow motion, or may portray a distorted perception of time in describing a situation.

coordination .02
Motor coordination is impaired.

motor performance .06
Ability to perform motor tasks, movements, and other reactions.

distance judgement .07
Ability to judge distance is impaired.

Also Available from LEXIS® Law Publishing:

The single most powerful resource a prosecutor or police investigator can have to prosecute DWI cases!

Investigation and Prosecution of DWI and Vehicular Homicide
John B. Kwasnoski, Gerald N. Partridge, John A. Stephen
$100 (# 64345; 1 volume, hardbound, copyright 1998)
    (Sales tax, shipping and handling not included.)

A comprehensive resource, **Investigation and Prosecution of DWI and Vehicular Homicide** equips prosecutors, police investigators, toxicologists and accident reconstructionists with the knowledge and skills needed to win convictions in vehicular homicide, and DWI, OUI, and DUI cases.

This how-to guide is packed with essential legal, investigation, and trial tips that police and prosecutors need to overcome defense strategies. The single volume includes:

- Checklists for processing the crash scene
- Case examples and corresponding accident reconstruction testimony
- Use of autopsy and medical reports in the driver identification case
- Hands-on techniques for establishing probable cause and obtaining samples of chemical tests
- Tips on developing exhibits that impact jurors
- Visible cues of impairment that can increase the detection of impaired drivers

Two battle-tested prosecutors and a national expert in accident reconstruction have collaborated to make this manual into a road map for proving guilt. You'll get a thorough understanding of the respective roles of prosecutors, police investigators, toxicologists, and accident reconstructionists in all aspects of DWI-related cases including:

- Locating and questioning witnesses
- Gathering information from the roadway and from the vehicles involved
- Dealing with expert testimony, including cross examination
- Introducing the DRE officer's evaluation testimony to the jury
- Cross examining the defendant
- Sentencing advocacy

Summary Table of Contents:
    Ch 1. The DWI Offense
    Ch 2. DWI Evidence
    Ch 3. Implied Consent
    Ch 4. Arrest and Custody
    Ch 5. Technical Investigation
    Ch 6. Accident Reconstruction
    Ch 7. Toxicology
    Ch 8. Pre-Trial
    Ch 9. Trial
    Appendices

"This book is must reading for any member of law enforcement investigating or prosecuting DWI and vehicular homicide cases. The authors have distilled their decades of experience into a practical and comprehensive manual that will assist police and prosecutors of every level of experience. I recommend this book highly."—**Vincent Bugliosi (former LA prosecutor; author of Helter Skelter and Outrage).**

To order, call toll free: 800/562-1197 FAX: 800/643-1280.

"Winning the DWI Crash Case"
A 1-Day Nationally Acclaimed
Police-Prosecutor Training Seminar

Instructors John B. Kwasnoski and Gerald N. Partridge, co-authors of *Investigation and Prosecution of DWI and Vehicular Homicide* and the *Officer's DUI Handbook*, conduct training nationwide for police and prosecutors.

What law enforcement professionals around the country say about "Winning the DWI Crash Case":

"By far the best class I have ever taken on the subject matter. If a department wants to increase its conviction rate, this is the class to take."—Detective William Refairn, Training Officer, Las Vegas, NV PD.

"The best I've attended. Renewed my motivation and enthusiasm."—Scott M. Muller, Syracuse, NY PD.

"In 23 years as a state trooper, this was by far the best 8-hour course I ever attended."—Lt. David Boyt, Georgia State Patrol.

"All technical investigators and DREs should take this training. Excellent."—Trooper Glen Swanson, Iowa State Patrol.

"Extremely good. Short, concise, and insightful. I particularly enjoyed the surviving cross examination for experts/police officers. The best 1-day seminar I've seen."—Gary R. Booker, DUI Team Chief, Chief Assistant DA, Clark County, NV.

"This is the strongest team of police and prosecutor trainers I've ever experienced. Their training methods are innovative, their teaching style is entertaining, and the instruction is as 'nuts and bolts' as it gets."—Larry Todd, Assistant Solicitor, Ninth Judicial Circuit, South Carolina.

"… the best in the country … From crash to courtroom these experts can help you make your case as tight as possible. Even seasoned veterans can learn new techniques."—Sarah Ritterhoff, Prosecutor, 5th Judicial Circuit, FL.

For information on sponsoring a seminar, contact:

Legal Sciences, Inc., 51 Nash Hill Road, Ludlow, MA
Fax: 319/653-6533 Phone: 319/653-3000

Also Available from LEXIS® Law Publishing:

Just Updated! Now including Sample Driving Records!

Prior Convictions in DUI Prosecutions
American Prosecutors Research Institute's National Traffic Law Center
$100   (# 61441; copyright 1997; 1058 pages, softbound + 1998 Supplement 368 pages, paperbound)
(Sales tax, shipping and handling not included.)

While proving a DUI is often hard, it is easy compared with obtaining the required documentation to prove a prior DUI conviction from another state. *Prior Convictions in DUI Prosecutions* will ease the burden of this difficult and time-consuming task. This important resource collects all the information a law enforcement professional needs to obtain a certified record of a prior out-of-state DUI conviction. This process used to be prohibitive for a prosecutor's office with limited time and resources. Not any more. This book gathers in one place all the hard-to-obtain information—for every state!

Assembled by the American Prosecutors Research Institute in conjunction with The National Traffic Law Center and published by LEXIS® Law Publishing, *Prior Convictions in DUI Prosecutions* shows you how to obtain out-of-state driving records. It explains how to obtain certified copies of conviction from the convicting court. And it provides numerous case law citations interpreting each state's DUI law, as well as the text of DUI statutes of every state from 1988 through 1997. Now including sample driving records for most states!

Summary Table of Contents:
   Introduction
   DUI/DWI State Statute Citations
   DUI/DWI State Statutes Included in This Manual
   Sample Form: Requesting DUI/DWI Court Conviction Records
   Sample Form: Department of Motor Vehicles Request for Driving Records
   Sample Driving Records

To order, call toll free: 800/562-1197 FAX: 800/643-1280

9116